Power through Acceptance

the Secret of Serenity

Gordon Powell

Power through Acceptance

the Secret of Serenity

Gordon Powell

CHRISTIAN HERALD BOOKS
Chappaqua, New York

*Dedicated
to
LOWELL THOMAS
whose letter of invitation
brought us to a whole new
ministry in America and whose
influence as a leading layman
in our congregation here
has been a blessing.*

Power through Acceptance

the Secret of Serenity

Gordon Powell

INTRODUCTION
By Dr. Norman Vincent Peale

IN OUR uptight era an increasing number of people are plagued and made unhappy and even ill by tension and worry. And in many cases effectiveness as persons is reduced by such emotional problems. This book, *Power through Acceptance–The Secret of Serenity*, is bound, therefore, to do an immense amount of good in alleviating prevailing troubles.

The late Dr. Smiley Blanton, a famous practicing psychiatrist and widely read author, said, "Anxiety is the great modern plague." He believed that the vast resources of psychological medicine, as well as those of Christianity should be mustered in joint attack upon the powerful emotional enemies of human well-being.

It is not surprising, therefore, that a considerable body of literature dealing with anxiety-tension has developed over recent years. Psychiatrists, psychologists, ministers and others working in the healing disciplines have, out of a profound concern, produced a sizable collection of articles and books dealing with this problem. Many such publications are indeed effective and some may be appraised as classics in the field. In this latter category most certainly must be included the writings of Dr. Gordon Powell, and particularly this present volume.

As a result of his extraordinary work in human problems,

Gordon Powell became probably the most celebrated minister in Australia. He was successively pastor of two of the outstanding churches in that country, St. Stephen's Presbyterian Church in Sydney, and the famed Scots Church in Melbourne. Always he attracted huge congregations, and his midweek noonday service in Sydney, designed especially for business people, was said to be the largest attended such regular religious meeting in the world. By popular request he preached frequently in my pulpit at Marble Collegiate Church in New York, and also appeared in distinguished pulpits in the United States, England and Canada.

A reason for his wide following, in addition to his acknowledged preaching ability, was largely Dr. Powell's remarkable skill in addressing his thinking to practical human needs. Not only was he sensitively aware of the pervasive extent of personal problems, but he was by nature equipped to relate to the individual who needed understanding and qualified help in dealing with fear, tension and related maladies. Dr. Powell studied intensively in the field of mental health and psychological understanding and became one of the best trained and sought after counselors in Australia.

His proven skills in personal counseling, as might be expected, became involved in his preaching. His strong interest in people and their possibilities for improvement was reflected in his pulpit talks to such an extent that his sermons and services of public worship took on to some extent the element of a group counseling experience for a large congregation. The therapeutic effect of such worship forms was attested by the thousands who found satisfying answers to their problems and new life emotionally and spiritually under his ministry.

Gordon Powell has been a personal friend for many years, but long before I met him I heard increasingly of the loving and healing influence this gifted and dedicated physician of souls had on the lives of people.

I became, of course, an appreciative reader of his books from which I derived definite personal help and inspiration.

He reached me by the same gentle but strongly believing persuasiveness that brought so many to the realization that in Christ the Savior are to be found all necessary resources for new life and personal victory over self defeating weakness. I discovered early in our friendship that while Dr. Powell is eminently qualified in the psychological approach to human problems, his message is soundly based on Jesus Christ and the Bible-centered gospel of salvation. The Holy Spirit working in the individual in Dr. Powell's teaching leads to true healing and life-changing power. He directs people to Jesus and persuades them to allow our Lord to perform the healing of their souls. And this, of course, leads to new health of mind and body.

The reader will, I am sure, find Dr. Powell's writing style to be a delight. His sentences march forward in orderly manner and sequence, like soldiers moving toward a goal. He writes for every man and every woman in words and concepts that are not only clearly understandable, but which also have impact upon the heart no less than upon the mind. His writing is in essence a form of talking as friend to friend. The reader soon becomes aware that this writer, whose thoughts and words he is following, is one who loves people, and in the name of Jesus Christ wants to help them.

Dr. Powell's books are actually workable and practical manuals of spiritual experience and new life. The principles which he carefully and interestingly outlines will work when worked as thousands of his readers will agree.

This present book will go far toward bringing to the reader the peace of God which passes understanding. It is a book for this uptight, worry-filled era and will, I am sure, bless anyone who reads and practices its inspired teachings.

—NORMAN VINCENT PEALE
New York
September 1976

PREFACE

"WHAT can you do about anxiety?"

My visitor, a business executive in his early forties, sat bolt upright on the edge of the chair. Beads of perspiration stood out on his upper lip and his forehead. His hands were clenched so tightly the knuckles showed white.

"What makes you anxious?" I asked.

"That's the trouble," he replied. "I can't name any particular cause. There's just a black cloud of fear all the time. The more I try to break clear the worse it seems to get. My nerves are at breaking point."

"You do seem pretty run down," I sympathized. "What about a vacation?"

"I've just come back from a month away. I thought I was better, but I've only been back at work a week and I'm worse than ever."

"What about psychiatric treatment?" I queried.

"I've been going to Dr.—— for nearly twelve months now." (The psychiatrist he named is an excellent man and a good friend of mine.) "He gave me some shock treatment and lately has had me on some of these new drugs. They seem to alleviate the trouble, but after a time it all comes back again. As a matter of fact he sent me along to you. Oh, I'd forgotten! I'm sorry—he gave me a letter for you. Here it is."

The letter introduced the patient and gave a brief outline of his history, indicating how I might be able to help.

"He suggests we discuss the spiritual answer to your problem," I said as I folded the letter again.

"That seems to be the idea."

"Perhaps you had better tell me something of your spiritual history then."

"Yes, I suppose I should," said my visitor. He hesitated and then broke off at a tangent. "Did you read that article on 'Stress' in the *Reader's Digest* some time back?"

"Yes, why?"

"It really frightened me. You may recall that it was all about Dr. Hans Selye, the head of some medical institute in Montreal. He has been making experiments for many years and has proved that our general health depends to a great extent on the pituitary and adrenal glands. If you suffer from a chill the glands will constrict the arteries to raise the blood pressure and provide greater warmth. When bacteria invades the body these glands produce inflammation which helps to ward off disease. If there is injury they act to hasten the clotting of blood, at the same time reducing blood pressure and increasing blood sugar to provide energy."

"You seem to have an excellent memory of the article," I remarked.

"I've always been interested in this sort of thing," he went on. "I once had an ambition to be a doctor, but family finances didn't permit. Anyway, the point is as the doctor proves, to my way of thinking beyond any shadow of doubt, these glands go into action when stimulated by stress in the mind and if the stress is prolonged the glands break down and consequently the whole system goes to pieces. You see why the article frightened me. As it said, stress is the great killer. I know that is true, but I just can't get rid of stress in the mind. Reading this kind of thing has only added to my fears. Tell me, what is the secret of serenity?"

"It looks," I said, "as though we are back again at the point where we were a few minutes ago. What is the spiritual answer to the problem?"

My visitor then told me the story of his life. In doing so he admitted that in recent years, while business and family responsibilities accumulated, he had allowed himself to become seriously under-nourished spiritually.

As I listened to his story and watched him making an effort to relax, the chorus of an old song kept coming back to me: "A contented mind is a blessing kind." One of the greatest blessings which the Christian faith confers on its followers is the blessing of a serene spirit gained through the power of acceptance.

Some people say a Christian should not be contented, he ought to be concerned. Certainly a Christian who is not alarmed by the evils of the modern world and anxious to do something about them, is not worthy of the name. But in my experience one of the evils confronting us is the tragic number of people like my business executive friend whose lives, in the midst of our modern civilization, are full of that very stress which is one of the prime enemies of health.

It has been proved over and over again that psychiatric treatment, important and effective as it is in cases where it is the appropriate therapy, cannot produce lasting results if the problem is basically spiritual. Many psychiatrists refer such patients to church for the only treatment adequate to root out the tensions of the soul.

So it was that my visitor that day, somewhat to his surprise, had been sent by a medical man to a minister. In terms of his own special need I talked to him along the lines of certain chapters in this book. Indeed, because he is only one of many hundreds, and we can't give the time we should to all who seek our aid, I felt this book had to be written. In my files are scores of letters from patients like the man described above, bearing ample evidence that the spiritual approach, the power which derives from accepting Christ and then accepting ourselves, is the supreme answer to the problem of tension.

Tension does so much harm in so many directions it would be difficult to list them all, let alone go into detail. However, there are two forms of it which we strike so often I feel I must refer to them here. Parents of children in their late teens are sometimes distressed because the children seem rebellious, even showing signs of hatred. The problem is often accentuated in the case of only children. To a large extent I believe it can be explained in terms of tension. The teenager is feeling insecure and tense because he has to leave the security of home and face the world. The problem is complicated by this fear being an unconscious one. He looks to his parents for security just when they are feeling tense because they are afraid for him. They transfer their tension to him when that is the last thing he wants. So he replies with resentment and what appears to be hatred. He transfers his own tension back to them and a vicious circle is created. In the natural course of events the young person finds his place in the world and the tension passes, but sometimes there is tragedy before that can happen. How much better it is when the parents, by discovering the spiritual answer to the problem, transfer serenity instead of tension. Then they prove again that "the family that prays together, stays together."

Again, the disease of compulsive alcoholism undoubtedly stems from unresolved tension in the mind.

This book has been written primarily for all battling with the problem of tension. It is also written for the average Christian believer. Unless we have serenity, the courage to change and the power to accept what we cannot change, we must ask ourselves whether we have entered the full Christian experience. Without "the peace of God which passeth all understanding" we cannot continue for long to do effective work for the Lord. Indeed we might do considerable harm. On the other hand if we possess it, we can convey it to others and so bring them inestimable blessing. We must pass on our spiritual blessings, if our inner life is to remain strong and serene.

The secret of peace of mind and spiritual serenity is really remarkably simple. Perhaps that is why so many miss this blessing today. We have been trained to think that anything immensely valuable must be extremely complicated and very costly. Christian serenity is neither. It is one of God's greatest gifts to those who come to a true understanding of Christian faith.

NOTE ON THE AMERICAN EDITION

Billy Graham had a problem on the night of Saturday, March 22, 1969. He was on his way back to his hotel in Melbourne, Australia, after the next to the last meeting of his Crusade in Victoria. He said to me, as the chairman of the organizing committee, "Can you help me? I have announced that I will preach on forgiveness at the final meeting tomorrow, but I don't have any address. Out of your ministry can you recall instances of people who have sought and found forgiveness?"

As we talked about it in the car I remembered that this book, simply called *The Secret of Serenity* in Australia, began with the story of a young woman who felt she had sinned and wanted cleansing from her sense of guilt.

Having dropped Billy at the hotel, I went back to my church and found a copy of the book. I marked the pages concerned, returned and left it with him.

Next afternoon on a day of beautiful sunshine, Billy preached to 85,000 people in the Melbourne Cricket Ground. His address began with the story of the young woman told here in chapter one and it contained several other quotations from the book.

Some months later Dr. Sherwood Wirt, then editor of *Decision* magazine, published "Accepting Power Over Sin," the ninth chapter under the heading, "The Sin That Won't Let Up."

Several of my other books have been published in the United States, but this is the first time this one on serenity has appeared in this country.

Since the book was originally written in Australia in the midst of a very busy ministry—over 3000 people worshipped every week in St. Stephen's Macquarie St. Sydney in those days—it contains a number of local references which would be confusing to American readers. These have largely been eliminated. Otherwise this is substantially the same book which, under God, has brought a new serenity to many readers.

The original Preface above contains a reference to the views of Dr. Hans Selye. His medical research has proved, at least according to the media, that "stress is the great killer." In more recent years Dr. Selye, who is Professor and Director of the Institute of Experimental Medicine and Surgery in the University of Montreal, has written many articles and books to show that stress need not be an enemy. One of his books, published in 1974, had the title, *Stress Without Distress*.

As Dr. Selye now emphasizes, without some stress life would lose its zest. It would become unbearably dull. Every human being needs stimulation to come alive and "raise consciousness." But we are all different and each has to find his own "optimum stress level."

Dr. Selye himself has worked all his adult life from 4 A.M. or 5 A.M. until 6 P.M. but he has enjoyed it and not found it "stressful." He has always had a purpose, to make a worthy contribution to medical science, to heal people sick and in pain and "to earn his neighbor's love."

Now in his late sixties he still works these long hours serenely. To combat the physical decay of encroaching age he keeps his muscles trim by swimming, or racing round the McGill campus on a bicycle at five in the morning! A calculated use of stress is keeping him from growing old.

I applaud him for this while accepting the fact that I am made differently and prefer to take my exercise later in the day. When possible I like to sunbathe, something which I find very conducive to peace of mind and physical well-being.

With all this, my experience as a minister makes me concerned about the stress caused by mental and spiritual factors. In this book I have tried to show that these cannot be dealt with by physical exercises, or by taking pills or medicines, all of which may have their importance at the proper time and in the proper circumstances. Spiritual stress can only be dealt with at the spiritual level. There is a wonderful answer to this in the Christian faith.

I wish to express my gratitude to Christian Herald Books for bringing out this revised and updated version of *The Secret of Serenity* in America, and Dr. Norman Vincent Peale, our neighbor and good friend, for his generous introduction. Also I thank Mrs. Norman Vincent Peale whose faith and positive thinking brought us all together.

—*G.P.*

CONTENTS

Chapter One

ACCEPTING THE PAST

SEVERAL years ago a young lady, who felt she had committed sin, wrote to me saying there were four questions to which she badly needed answers. In due time she came in for an interview and, because her problem is shared by many others, I obtained her permission to publish our discussion.

This girl was brought up by parents whose moral outlook was possibly a little narrow. As often happens in such a home, she had no training in matters of sex. Then she met a young man and fell in love. The romance prospered and they began to make plans for marriage. As the courtship developed they indulged in petting which lead to a more serious involvement and this resulted in a deep sense of guilt. This was accentuated when she thought of her work as a Sunday school teacher. The problem became really acute when there was a quarrel and the engagement was broken off. In the depth of her misery and sense of guilt she wrote her letter posing the four questions. They were:

1. Should I keep my job as a Sunday school teacher?
2. How do you think I can best atone for the wrong I have done?
3. Do you think I should ever marry anyone? I have reached a stage where I could not be happy with anyone who is not a keen Christian, so possibly am not worthy of anyone like that.
4. If I do marry anyone, should I tell him of these things?

As we discussed her problem in detail I told her I found the answer to the first question comparatively easy. Since she repented of her sin, I felt she should certainly continue to serve in the sphere to which she had felt called. If only those who had never sinned were permitted to serve in the church there would be no office-bearers in the church at all. The day Jesus issued the challenge, "Let him that is without sin cast the first stone," not a man could face him.

When it came to the question of atoning for the wrong committed I asked her to consider who it was she felt had been wronged, the young man, herself, God or somebody else. Giving the matter some thought she eventually made this interesting answer, "The danger of a conviction of wrong-doing is that one starts to hate—God, for the way he has made us; our parents for the things they have not taught us; the person who has wronged us. Perhaps it is the penetration of that hate which is the biggest sin of all." I felt that she was now getting down to the real cause of her trouble. The physical expression of affection between two people who are deeply in love and who plan to marry, if kept within proper limits, is not a sin. The danger is that when it goes beyond these proper limits it stirs up fires which are difficult to control. If marriage follows all may be well, but if something goes wrong, young people are left with a tumult of emotions which torture them.

What can be done about it? Nothing can undo the past. But God can do great things with the spirit which is tortured by the past and sincerely repentant of it. This girl now saw that her real sin was hatred—hatred of the young man, hatred of her parents, hatred of God. It was the natural and vicious reaction of a soul that has been hurt. Yet nothing is more destructive than hatred, especially hatred of God, because in such hatred there is fear, torture and disintegration. It destroys peace, harmony and strength. The greatest thing that we can then say is, "God be merciful to me, a sinner. Create in me a clean heart. Renew in me a right spirit." Atonement is made by this new spirit. Forgiveness and love on our part replace the disintegrating force of hatred.

Having reached this point the answer to her next question became clearer. Of course it would be right to marry someone else because she was now a new personality. The past was over and done with. God can't "unhappen" the past, but because he himself has provided atonement for it he can accept it and take away its power to drag us down. Indeed, as we shall see later, he can give us the power to profit from the mistakes of the past.

Her final question I found the most difficult of all. I think it a good working principle in married life that husbands and wives should share everything honestly and have no secrets. However, it has been our experience in pastoral counselling that when an unfortunate past, and especially a sinful one, is dwelt upon, instead of strengthening the marriage it can sometimes destroy it. God has put our sin "behind his back." We should leave it there and not drag it out again to trouble ourselves or our partner. The whole point of this first chapter is that serenity comes by accepting the past. Let us live the full Christian life each day as it comes, like Paul, "forgetting the things which are behind." Has not God said, "Though your sins be as scarlet, they should be as white as snow"? Let us take him at his word.

It is now quite a few years since the young lady I have been describing faced her crisis. It is good to be able to report that in due course she met another young man of outstanding Christian character and is now very happily married. Her story illustrates the three main points I want to emphasize in regard to the power of acceptance as far as the past is concerned.

1

An unaccepted past is fatal to peace of mind.—It is useless to run away from our past. Before we can safely forget it, we have to face it and deal with it.

Thousands of people are living darkened, "mixed-up" lives today because they have never applied this truth to themselves. To take a vivid example we have the story which forms the starting point of Dr. Paul Tournier's fascinating volume, *A Doctor's Casebook in the Light of the Bible.*

Tournier is a physician in Geneva where he makes a special study of the relationship between spiritual factors and physical health. He has written many books on the subject. One day the wife of another doctor came to see him saying she was anxious about her husband's health. He was always over-tired and his nerves were constantly on edge, yet he had not taken a vacation in years, saying he could not afford it. She felt sure he was suffering from some deep and mysterious agony of mind. A year before he had spent several months in hospital with septicaemia. The trouble had begun with an unimportant local infection which had developed so seriously that the finest medical treatment and modern drugs had made little impression. When at last he was discharged, instead of going off for a much-needed convalescence, he had immediately hurled himself back into his work again as furiously as ever. His wife now feared a complete collapse and pleaded with Dr. Tournier to have a talk with him.

The sick doctor accepted Dr. Tournier's invitation and then poured out the story of his life. As a student he had committed a certain sin. One lapse led to others until he had become a slave to his weakness. He had harbored this evil thing in his heart and mind, never unburdening his soul to his wife or to the church, though outwardly he was a religious man. His incessant work was not merely a form of self-punishment, it was necessary to meet the financial commitments involved by his youthful folly. He fully realized that the torture in his mind was largely responsible for his wretched health and explained why the antibiotics had produced so little effect during his hospitalization. As they talked it over the two doctors agreed that every illness needed two diagnoses—the scientific which dealt with what was happening at the physical level, and the spiritual which

26

dealt with the "meaning" of the disease, and, therefore, in most cases, its causes. For some time the medical profession has recognized that the main causes of neurotic disease are mental and spiritual. A growing number share Dr. Tournier's view that organic, physical disease also has "spiritual meaning."

This man was sick because of sin. All the antibiotics in the world could not heal his tortured soul. Encouraged by Dr. Tournier he went back to his church, made confession of his sin and accepted the forgiveness of God. He also talked the matter over freely and frankly with his wife, which, in the special circumstances surrounding their case, was apparently the right thing to do. Then the two of them went off for a second honeymoon, and soon he found himself gloriously free from the past which had darkened his life and destroyed his health. As Tournier puts it, unforgiven sin "acts as a clog upon vitality." When forgiveness is accepted "there is a current of physical life which is re-established on contact with God." This brings me to my second main point.

2

It is only safe to accept the past when it has been dealt with at the spiritual level. —It would be easy enough to say, "The past is a burden to me. I will accept it in the mind, stop worrying about it and forget it." We are so made that we can't do that as both the young lady and the sick doctor discovered. We are merely pushing the problem down into the unconscious mind where it festers and destroys serenity and health. We have to face it and deal with it at the only level where it can be dealt with, namely the moral and spiritual level. We have to get right with God.

Volumes have been written on how man may "get right with God," but to me it is all summed up in the parable of the prodigal son, a story now so familiar to most of us that we miss its sublime truths. This young man, according to an ancient custom, persuaded his father to divide the family estate between them while the father still lived. When this was done the beneficiaries were in honor bound to care for the old people during their remaining days upon this earth. Regardless of this clear duty the boy went off to the bright lights of a distant city and squandered the money which he regarded as his own, but which was still actually his father's (as the elder brother later emphasized). This is what sin is. It is wasting the wealth which God has entrusted to us—our talents, gifts, time and substance.

Then the young man came to himself, or as Phillips translates, came to his senses. While the old theological argument is that man's natural state is a sinful one, the clear teaching of Jesus in this parable is that when a man comes to his true self, when he is in his right mind, he recognizes sin as sin and yearns to be free of it. Only the darkened mind wants to stay in a state of sin. When the theologians talked about "the Fall," they implied that man had once been on a higher level. Everything God made was good—including man. When the prodigal returned to "normal," he regained his moral and spiritual sanity and was willing to go back to his father whom he had so grievously wronged. There is also a hint that as a hired servant he was prepared to work and make restitution for the wrong he had done. But that was not required. As soon as the father heard his son's sincere confession he broke him off at once and ordered a sumptuous feast of celebration. All was forgiven as soon as the change of heart was recognized.

The young man said he had sinned against his father and against heaven. Like the rest of us he realized that when we do wrong, not only do we hurt our fellow human beings, but we hurt God. Only by a sincere repentance can we be brought back into a right relationship both with man and God. The great word of comfort which Jesus brought to us from this parable is this:—God is like the father who so quickly forgave his erring son. So God will forgive us, He will restore us and, indeed, make things better than ever before. Which brings me to the third main point.

God will accept our past and help us to profit from it.—The prodigal, to his surprise, found himself in the center of a celebration. Through the forgiving love of his father he was able to make an entirely new beginning. From the point of view of the family he had been "lost" and "dead." From the point of view of his own real life he had been lost, dead to all the finer things, the things which really satisfy and ultimately give meaning to our existence. Now he was born again. He was beginning an entirely new life.

Thanks to what we call the grace of God the past can lose its power over us, we can accept it in our minds and our emotions, and then with a new power from God we can begin to live as God meant us to live. One Sunday after the evening service I had a visit with a man whom I had not seen for eight years. I could not get over the change in him. The last time I had seen him he was wallowing in the misery of alcoholism. He told me that he had never actually reached the shoe polish stage, but he was very close to it and a total physical and mental wreck. Like the prodigal he came back to God, accepted divine forgiveness and "the power greater than himself." It warmed my heart just to look at him. He is a radiant Christian believer now and a living witness to the grace and power of God. He has returned from the far country and discovered something he might never have found otherwise, the spiritual power to win the victory in every area of life. Whatever suffering we have to face, whether through our own folly or not, God can help us to profit by it. This man today has a sympathy with other alcoholics, and he knows how to help them. Thereby he has discovered a new satisfaction never known before. By entering into this positive and constructive relationship with others his own life has been enriched.

Let me conclude with a delightful story which may serve to remind us that God not only forgives, but makes life better than ever. About a hundred years ago a girl who had been left an orphan in a remote German town, being in dire need, advertised a pianoforte recital. The posters stated that she was a pupil of the celebrated Hungarian pianist and composer Franz Liszt though this was quite untrue. You may imagine her horror when she heard that Liszt was actually coming to their town at the time of her recital and would certainly see the posters. In anguish of soul she began to picture all kinds of dire consequences. Then taking her courage in her hands she sought an interview with the great man when he arrived on the day before her recital. In his presence she sobbed out her confession and awaited his rebuke. Liszt said to her, "You have done wrong, but we all make mistakes, and then the only thing left to do is to be sorry. I think you are sorry. Let me hear you play." This was almost too much for the girl, playing in front of the master himself. At first she stumbled quite a little, but as she won more confidence she played better. Liszt corrected her in one or two points and then he said, "My dear, I have now instructed you a little. You are a pupil of Liszt. You may go on with your concert tomorrow night, and the last item will be played, not by the pupil, but by the master."[1]

God is like that. When we come back to him in sincere contrition for the past he fills our cup full, even to overflowing.

So it is that our first step on the road to serenity is to learn how, with God's help, to accept the past. The right attitude to it in the mind can take the torture out of it. Indeed such an attitude can enable us to build a finer future not merely in spite of, but because of, the unfortunate past. Before we do that we must learn to accept the present.

---

[1] Paraphrased from *500 Tales to Tell Again* by H. L. Gee (Epworth Press).

Chapter Two

ACCEPTING THE PRESENT

ONE of the greatest spiritual forces I ever met was a humble little woman who lived in Port Adelaide in South Australia. When my wife and I went to our first church there, we met all sorts of people who asked us had we met Liz Clouston. It was apparent that to a remarkable degree the life of the church revolved around the personality of this woman. We began to picture her as strong, tall, dominant. Imagine our surprise when at last we met her to find that she was less than five feet high, living in a cottage with ceilings so low we felt we had to bow our heads. On one corner of the cottage was built a grocery store so cramped for space that if more than two or three customers entered the others had to wait outside. The store was situated in a part of Port Adelaide which had suffered cruelly in the depression. More than half the men were unemployed. Liz Clouston was so kind-hearted she continued to supply groceries whether people could pay or not. Not all of them knew that in a back room of the cottage was a sister permanently bed-ridden and in constant pain. Another sister lived with them, but she too was frequently laid aside with sickness.

Struggling under such a burden Liz Clouston would have been only human if she had moaned and complained at her fate. Instead she was the brightest person one could possibly meet. She always had a cheerful smile and was ready with a joke. In spite of all she had to do at the store and in the home, she found time to work like a beaver for the women's guild, and the church generally. We soon discovered that the church was in debt and in due course decided to make an appeal for $1,000. It seems a small enough amount these days, but in a poverty-stricken church with most families still in debt it seemed overwhelming. On the night the appeal was launched one of the first to come forward was Liz Clouston with her "widow's mite" as she called it. Actually it was quite a substantial sum. I shall never forget the look of radiance on her face as she offered her gift to God, or her joy a few weeks later when I was able to tell her the whole amount had been subscribed. Whether or not she realized her own example had played a great part in the success of the appeal I cannot say, but this I do know, she found her greatest satisfaction in serving Christ and his kingdom in her own home and through the church. Hers was a truly victorious life, and two years after these events I discovered the secret of it. With her usual smile she said to me, "Mr. Powell, one of these days I would like you to preach a sermon on my favorite text, 'Godliness with contentment is great gain.'"

How many people today spoil their lives because they have not learned to control mental stress? Instead of being stalwarts in the battle for righteousness, they are incapacitated to a great degree. Contrary to all their desire they have to withdraw from the fight. Therefore, I maintain, if Christian faith can show the way to cope with stress in the mind, if it can produce a "place of central calm," it will be rendering a very great service. Perhaps Paul spoke even truer than he knew when he declared "Godliness with contentment is great gain."

1

To a great extent godly contentment consists in mentally accepting present circumstances which cannot be changed.—We all know people who are constantly making themselves sick and bringing gloom into the lives of those round about them by rebelling mentally against their circumstances. This rebellion builds up the mental stress which destroys health. That is why I prefer the Revised Version of Paul's statement (in Philippians 4), "I have learned, in whatsoever state I am, therein to be content." He was not content *with* his circumstances, but he had learned to be content *in* his circumstances. As a leading business man said during a public debate in our church hall, any man can bear enormous loads and fulfill endless duties provided he does not worry about them.

The Rev. Dr. Norman Vincent Peale has been described as "not a man, but an industry." After forty years he still preaches every Sunday to one of the largest congregations in New York City. His best-selling books, radio and TV programs bring in literally thousands of letters a week. Some 500 people are employed to produce *Guideposts* magazine which is read by 9,000,000 readers every month. Another large staff at the Foundation for Christian Living here in Pawling where I am now typing these words, sends out millions of his sermons to addresses in 130 countries round the world. One of Dr. Peale's journalistic activities is a question and answer column syndicated to 250 newspapers. In reply to one question, "You are a very busy man. How do you keep from getting tired?" his extraordinary answer was:

"By keeping busy. By being interested in everything. By trying to do some good and by getting a lot of fun out of life. Sure, I get a good healthy tiredness. Then I go to bed and sleep. The next morning I feel enthusiastic and ready to go again. One of my favorite Bible texts may explain my philosophy, 'They that wait upon the Lord shall renew their strength.'"

Dr. Peale's book on *The Power of Positive Thinking* has been read by millions. He practices what he preaches so he does not use up energy nor develop undue stress in his mind by fretting about circumstances he does not like. He faces constant criticism which would break any other man, but he does not become bitter about it. Refusing to wear himself out with negative emotions, he accepts circumstances as they are and goes to work on them enthusiastically.

Consider one circumstance which troubles many people, especially men—lack of height. Jesus advised us to accept this kind of circumstance and not worry about it. In the Sermon on the Mount he said, "Which of you by taking thought can add one cubit unto his stature?" I believe that Jesus was here enunciating a general principle to the effect that a Christian has a duty to avoid worry about those things he cannot change. Nevertheless let us consider two examples which illustrate the literal truth of what Jesus said.

One of my predecessors in the Collins St. Independent Church in Melbourne was the Rev. Ernest James, a man little more than five feet high and boyish looking as well. Like many Congregational ministers he preferred to wear an ordinary collar and tie. One day he was walking up the hill in Collins St. when the driver of a horse-wagon heavily laden with bricks realized that the hill was too much for his horses. He shouted to Ernest James, "Say, boy, shove a brick under the wheel will you?" Mr. James told the story against himself from the pulpit and often appeared to joke about his lack of inches. Yet his wife told me that to his dying day he felt a bitterness about his shortness. The pity of it is he did not realize that so far from being a handicap his shortness probably contributed to the very great success he had in Collins St. He came to the church in 1917 when it had been vacant for some time and had reached the lowest point in its history. I remember seeing the record of the Sunday offerings for that year and on at least one occasion the total for a morning service was less than $2. Frequently it did not reach $4. This in a church built to seat 1,250 people. Yet within six years Ernest James had brought such life back to that dying church that people would line up in Collins St. long before the service anxious to secure a seat. His lack of inches did not prevent him achieving that kind of success, any more than a similar handicap held back men like John Wesley, Julius Caesar or Napoleon Bonaparte.

Knowing these things I had always assumed that these men had succeeded in spite of their handicap. A statement by Gen. Carlos Romulo, the little man who so nobly represented the Philippines in the United Nations made me realize that shortness could actually be an asset. As he put it people, especially men, feel a kind of resentment in the presence of tall people. Unconsciously they don't like to be "looked down on." On the other hand tall people are free from that resentment. As they look down physically on others they tend to feel friendliness toward them. When Romulo woke up to this truth he declared "I'm glad I'm a little guy." He went further and declared that he was glad he represented a "little nation." The big nations are often suspicious and jealous of each other. The little nations can sometimes exercise more influence in world affairs because they are little nations. So it is that Romulo by mentally accepting the circumstance of his lack of inches learned to "glory in his infirmity," to use another phrase from Paul. Instead of this circumstance being a source of negative emotions for Romulo, it has become a source of positive emotions and strength.

Worrying about our circumstances won't get us anywhere and might do considerable harm. On the other hand if we accept them and go on to do the best with what we have, we might find that circumstances which we regard as evil are actually great blessings. Some years ago I corresponded with Mr. K. H. Blaxland the great grandson of the explorer, Gregory Blaxland who led the party which included Wentworth and Lawson in the first successful attempt to find a way over the Blue Mountains in New South Wales. Returning from their triumph they were each rewarded with a grant of a 1,000 acres. You may imagine Blaxland's feelings when he saw his two companions take up rich country while he was given an area south of Sydney so poor that "it would not feed a wallaby." There seems little doubt that a quarrel between his brother John and Governor Macquarie was at the root of this injustice. Gregory was so disgusted that he sold his rights for 50 cents an acre. That land today, between

Cronulla and Sylvania, is virtually a part of Greater Sydney and is worth millions. Had Blaxland held on to his land his descendants would have been extremely wealthy people. This to me is a parable of life. Too often we give up in disgust and grow bitter because of what we regard as unjust circumstance, when if we would only battle with it great things might be achieved. Many of our so-called handicaps are really wonderful assets if we could only see them in their true light. Let us then accept our circumstances and build up from there.

2

The godly mind is a contented mind.—To be contented with all our circumstances, of course, could be a very bad thing. Nothing angered Jesus more than to see people concerned only with their own spiritual and material comfort shutting their eyes to the great needs of humanity all round them. Few parables are more telling than the vivid picture of the rich man and the beggar, Lazarus (Luke 16). Yet Jesus himself often went off alone to pray on a mountain or in a desert place that he might regain inner serenity and peace. If he needed to do that in order to find strength to continue the battle against evil, how much more do we need to do so?

Or consider King David. Few men led a more active life, or battled more resolutely against evil things than he in his younger days. That was the time when he lived by his own 23rd Psalm.

The Lord is my shepherd; I shall not want.
He maketh me to lie down in green pastures:
He leadeth me beside the still waters.
Because of this inner spiritual content, he could face all kinds of adversity in his outward circumstances.

I want to conclude with the story of a wonderful victory over circumstances achieved in Sydney. I will preface it with another quotation from Dr. Paul Tournier:

"If the cripple revolts and complains, he cripples his spirit also, and shuts himself off from outside contacts, becoming hard and inadaptable. But insofar as he succeeds, helped by his faith, in accepting his infirmity, he relaxes and finds in himself new energy to live in spite of everything, and often an extraordinary capacity to overcome his difficulties. I say 'helped by his faith' because I am becoming more and more convinced that on the human level acceptance is all but impossible."[1]

Georgie Lane grew up at Riverstone in the country 30 miles from Sydney. As a boy he attended the Presbyterian Church and Sunday school. He was a normal, healthy Australian boy. Then at the age of 12 he was stricken with a vicious form of arthritis. Before long he had lost his eyesight and his hearing. As though that were not enough he became almost completely paralyzed. He has been like that for 7 years. About the only thing left to him is his voice—and a wonderful spirit. The Apostle Paul said that he had learned in whatsoever state he was therein to be content. Such circumstances as these, surely, would have tested even the magnificent spirit of Paul to the limit. They certainly tested Georgie Lane, but he has risen triumphant over everything. The only way visitors can communicate with him as he lies there on his special hospital bed is to write messages on his chest. All kinds of famous people have made pilgrimages to his bed. One of them was Ken Rosewall, the Davis Cup tennis star. Rosewall was amazed to find that Georgie knew more about his own tennis scores than he did himself. Georgie has retained his interest in everything and talks brightly and volubly about it all. In spite of total darkness, total silence and almost complete paralysis he is determined to live widely.

Thousands of other people with one tenth of his troubles moan about their afflictions, complaining that life has been unfair to them. They blame God and refuse to believe in him. Georgie Lane has never lost his faith for all his sufferings. Beside his bed he keeps the text:

"Come unto me all ye that labor and are heavy laden, and I will give you rest."

On the day Georgie Lane was received into full membership

[1] *A Doctor's Case Book in the Light of the Bible.* (S.C.M. Press.)

of the church and took communion, he said, "It is a great feeling to be one of the big family of the friends of Jesus."

His life illuminates the two texts, "I have learned in whatsoever state I am therein to be content;" "Godliness with contentment is great gain." Georgie Lane learned to accept present circumstances. In doing so he found serenity which enabled him to win an amazing victory.

Having considered the importance of eliminating stress by cultivating the mental attitude which accepts the past and the present, let us next consider the need to accept the future.

Chapter Three

ACCEPTING THE FUTURE

WHEN people live in constant dread of the future, serenity
and joy soon disappear from their lives.

I think of a man who was a clerk in a city business house.
As a young man he had attended church fairly regularly, but
then he drifted away. In due course he married, but after
several years of domestic bliss his wife died. In his loneliness
he rushed into another marriage which was a disappointment. His grief and worry told upon his nerves so that his
work became a burden to him. He made frequent mistakes so
that there was trouble at the office. He became a victim of
insomnia which, of course, increased his tension and made
things most difficult for his adolescent son and daughter,
who were already having some difficulty in becoming adjusted to a stepmother. Frequent scenes at home further
undermined the father's health until he was at the point of
total collapse. It is hardly surprising that in this state he
became obsessed with the alarming state of the world generally. He was constantly predicting the Third World War,
apparently determined to make everybody else as gloomy as
himself. One day he said to his daughter, "I hope you never
have any children." It was at this point that the family sought
psychiatric and spiritual aid. Abnormal fear of the future can
undermine anybody's sanity. Not only was this man living in

constant dread of what would happen to the world, but he had convinced himself that death would strike again at his own family circle and that, when it did, his own health and sanity, already seriously impaired, would totally collapse. In this latter regard his fear was actually producing the very result he was so anxious to avoid.

What is the spiritual answer to this problem? One woman I know found the answer in the farewell message of Moses to the children of Israel. It came about in this way. Living in a country district, she and her husband had faced bad seasons, much sorrow and worry until her health broke down and she ended up in hospital. In the next bed was a woman with whom she found she had much in common. They became great friends and corresponded regularly long after our patient had left hospital. In that town was an energetic group of young people belonging to the Christian Endeavor. Part of their community service was to take flowers to the patients in hospital. With each bunch of flowers came some helpful text from the Bible. One day they brought to the woman still in hospital the text (from Deuteronomy 33:25) "As thy days, so shall thy strength be." She found it a help in her own life and then sent it on to her friend who wrote and told me how again and again this text had come to her just when she needed it most. Many a time she dreaded what lay ahead, but then she steadied herself with the words, "As thy days, so shall thy strength be," and the thought that each morning God gives us strength for the new day.

These were not just pious words spoken originally by some ancient preacher living within the peace and serenity of a sanctuary. They were spoken by that great old warrior Moses after a lifetime of battling with ruthless enemies, a stubborn and wayward people of his own, and not least the cruel desert. Only a man of phenomenal courage and character could have seen it through. What was his secret? When he knew the time had come to pass on into the great unknown, Moses shared his secret with his people:

As thy days, so shall thy strength be . . .
The eternal God is thy refuge,
     and underneath are the everlasting arms.

When we have this kind of faith it gives us courage to do three things about our fear of the future. The first is to face it.

1

Face it.—Some time ago I was preparing for a particular interview which I was convinced would be an ordeal. In spite of my attempts to control my feelings I was working myself into quite a state when I went to the kitchen to get a glass of water, my mouth being particularly dry. My wife had just received a missionary magazine in the mail. It was lying face downward on the kitchen table. The words printed on the back cover suddenly caught my attention:—

FEAR KNOCKED ON THE DOOR,
FAITH OPENED IT,
THERE WAS NOBODY THERE.

I felt better at once. The words prompted me to go to my study and to make it a matter of prayer. As I prayed, the words kept coming to me,

"Just leave it to Me."

I don't say that my fear was banished entirely, but it was so greatly reduced that my mind calmed down, became clearer, and I was able to prepare for the interview I dreaded. In some respects it was worse than I had anticipated, but the ultimate result was better than my highest hopes. I am sure that when we do have faith to "leave it to God," all things eventually work together for good. But if fear makes us run away then the last state is worse than the first.

An outstanding illustration of that was the case of a friend of ours living in Melbourne. One dark night she was suddenly attacked from behind. Her assailant threw her to the ground, seized her handbag and made off. Apart from a few bruises she was not harmed physically, but the effect on her mind was serious. Her nerve was so severely shaken that from then on she could not go out after dark. If she tried to do so terror would grip her and she would be unable to control her trembling limbs. After one or two attempts she gave up the struggle, hoping the feeling would pass. Instead it became worse. Since her life was now seriously cramped, she resolved to go for an extended vacation, hoping a complete change might break up this awful phobia.

One Sunday morning, she worshiped with us at St. Stephen's in Sydney. It so happened that I was preaching on the two disciples who walked the road to Emmaus after the crucifixion of their Lord. Grief-stricken and overwhelmed by a great fear, they had been joined by a Stranger. They felt better as they talked with him and then that night, as he broke bread with them, suddenly their eyes were opened and they knew him. Although he immediately vanished from their sight, they were changed men, realizing that their beloved Master was no longer dead, but alive for evermore, capable of walking with them and talking with them. Strengthened by that faith these two disciples who earlier had one thought only, and that was to put as much distance as possible between them and Jerusalem, now turned and *through the night* hurried back to the city, the place of such danger to them, to tell the good news to the disciples who still remained there.

Our friend listening to this sermon felt it was a message meant directly for her and resolved that, come what may, she would worship with us again that evening. She was staying in a northern suburb across Sydney harbor and it involved a lengthy walk along a tree-lined street. However, she came in while it was still twilight, knowing she could only get back by walking that street in total darkness. This act of faith meant that the evening service was worship with more meaning in it than she had experienced for a long time. Afterwards she walked home along that dark street in complete calm and next morning she wrote me a joyful letter in which she said this:

"I want to tell you what a wonderful relief it was this morning to awaken and feel I have once again got my self-respect back. Each morning for over six months I have awakened feeling so ashamed of myself at letting this fear take all the real joy and peace out of my life. I felt it was sapping my spiritual strength."

She escaped from the grip of her phobia when she faced it.

Previously she had tried to screw up her own courage to face it, but all she was doing was to increase the tension, so adding to the fascination and power of her fear. When, in the faith that the unseen Lord was walking beside her, she was able to hand over her fear to him, the tension was relieved, her natural courage prevailed and her "self-respect" returned.

Leslie Weatherhead in his *Prescription for Anxiety* recalls the story of the witch who was turned into a cat. A small boy fled from it terrified, only to find that it grew to the size of a calf and then to that of a house and followed him till he fell, unable to flee any further. Then he had to face it, and as he advanced towards it, it dwindled in size until finally it ran under the door of the witch's cottage and disappeared. In battling with the problem of fear the first important thing is to face up to it.

2

Hand your fear over to the Lord.—The second important thing, as we have already seen, is to hand the fear over to the Lord. If we hold it in our own minds and wrestle with it there we can only make it worse, but with God's help we can accept the situation mentally without allowing emotional reactions to precipitate the disaster we fear.

The story of Daniel in the lions' den is an excellent illustration of that. For some reason this story seems to create difficulties for those who claim to have a scientific attitude toward life. Yet to me it is a story which can quite simply be explained in scientific terms. After all most of us have seen lion-tamers at work. Many of them carry a whip, but what protection would a whip be against a really angry lion? No, there is something in the mental or spiritual power of the lion-tamer over the beasts around him. It was once explained to me by a scientist. Following certain experiments, they had proved that when a man is frightened of a horse, the horse is aware of it not just by "instinct," or the physical impact of trembling knees or hands, but because the man, being frightened, breathes out certain chemicals. These chemicals are produced by the effect of fright on the man's glands. Inhaled by the horse, they affect him. Whatever be the explanation, it is clear enough that a human being can easily transfer tension to an animal, and in the same way he can also communicate calmness and power.

In the case of Daniel, the prophet had such a serene faith in God that when he was cast into the den of lions he remained perfectly calm, believing that God would protect him. Daniel walked among the beasts like any lion-tamer. Next day when he was taken out and his enemies were thrown in we can picture the terror and the screaming. It would be an open invitation to any lion to attack!

God grant us the faith to hand our emotional turmoil over to him just as Daniel did. Many people claim to believe in God, but they lack a simple and practical trust in him. I think of a girl who came to see me once. She was a bundle of nerves, terrified of the future and in particular obsessed with the idea that she was going out of her mind. When I asked her what gave her that idea she said:

"I can't help feeling there is a weakness in the family. My father suffered from melancholia for several years before he died. It was awful. I'm like my father and I'm sure I'm going the same way."

To comfort her I began to talk about the spiritual answer to the problem, but it only seemed to make things worse. She burst out:

"That's the terrible part about it. Father was a religious man, and it did not stop him going like that. On his black days he used to go about quoting the Bible, 'Why art thou cast down, O my soul?' God did seem to have deserted him. His faith didn't save him from going crazy."

I then had to ask her was she so sure of his faith. Plenty of people can quote Scripture texts without having a real faith. I went on to explain that the very text which she had just quoted was of tremendous comfort and strength to me during the Second World War. The time had come for me to pack up and leave for active service. I did not know which day would be my last with my wife and the three little children we had at that time. For all I knew it might be the last I would ever see of them in this world. In spite of myself I was filled with an overpowering sense of depression. Then one afternoon as I was out walking, this text came to me, "Why art thou cast down, O my soul? Hope thou in God." My fear and depression lifted, and when bad times came again the memory of these words dispelled the dark clouds. It is little use just asking the question, "Why art thou cast down, O my soul?" That only intensifies the perplexity and misery. But go on to the great positive affirmation and what a difference it makes! "Hope thou in God." Hand all your fears over to him.

In those days of war it was very easy to fear that civilization was on the way to destruction, that the future was entirely dark. Troubled souls still feel convinced that mankind will shortly bring annihilation upon itself. But as has been well said, every new-born baby is proof that God has not yet lost faith in the human race. "Hope thou in God."

3

Accept God's help. —"Acceptance" is the key word in dealing with fear, the enemy of our serenity. First we must accept the situation in the mind without working ourselves into a frightful stew over what is likely to happen. It is so easy to picture the worst possible consequences and to become highly emotional about them, when there is every chance that they may not happen at all. A calm assessment of the possibilities, reasonable precautions, and then a handing over of the fear to God are the right ways to deal with fearful situations. Having done that, the true believer will go further and accept his help at the spiritual level to cope with the situation.

J. M. Dent in England was a bookbinder on a very modest salary. He was a man of vision and faith. He married on practically nothing and then, with a plant costing only $20, he set up as a publisher. He struggled on for years in debt, but with hope in his heart. Then came two staggering blows. After a lingering illness his wife died. Then a fire destroyed his premises, and he lost everything he possessed. Fifteen years of struggle had ended in sorrow, disaster and defeat. He had only one wish and that was to die. Fortunately he had a good friend named George Carter who believed in him still. George Carter was a grocer in a small way. He had little money himself, but while others spoke of J. M. Dent as being "washed up," Carter persuaded him to try again and helped to get him back on his feet. Before long Dent was publishing the "Temple Library" series of books, the "Pocket Shakespeare" and then the famous "Everyman" series. Successful and prosperous as he became, he never forgot his good friend George Carter who stood by him.

The Christian should never forget that he has a friend who stands by him, a friend who knows all about fear because he "set his face to go to Jerusalem," aware that the cross and death were waiting for him there. The faith that this risen Christ is beside him and is quite capable of controlling the future whatever evil may come, is a source of serenity and courage to many a humble Christian believer.

It is a paradox that the Christ who died upon the cross should be able to bring such comfort to those who fear suffering and death, yet so it is. Professor Arnold Toynbee, the great authority on world history, several years ago concluded his *magnum opus*, ten large volumes on the history of mankind. In these books he traced the rise and fall of civilization after civilization. He analysed the reasons why they rose and fell, the outside pressures, the internal corruption. Naturally we ask, will our civilization also crash to destruction? Toynbee's answer was "Not necessarily. It depends on the religious response we make to the dangerous situation in which we find ourselves." He then described a dream he had years ago—a dream which obviously made a deep spiritual impression upon him at the time and which was a source of comfort and inspiration ever after. In his dream he pictured himself in Ampleforth Abbey in Yorkshire. Above the altar is suspended from the ceiling a huge cross. In his dream

Professor Toynbee saw himself clinging to the foot of the cross. He heard a voice saying, "Amplexus, expecta." (Cling and wait). So Toynbee concluded his mighty study of history by giving this same message to mankind, afflicted as we are by all kinds of fears, "Cling to the cross and wait." The cross brings home to us the reality of the forgiving love of God and such "perfect love casteth out fear." Again the cross speaks to us of God's power to overcome—eventually—every kind of evil. In this faith let us learn the art of accepting the future.

Chapter Four

ACCEPTING OURSELVES

MANY people would be much more serene if they could only learn the art of accepting themselves as God made them. I think of a young man I knew some years ago. He was sent to us by a psychiatrist because of overwhelming feelings of inferiority. He had withdrawn almost entirely from normal society and, becoming more and more absorbed with his morbid thoughts about himself, was in grave danger of serious mental trouble. The psychiatrist thought it would help if he could mix in with the young people at the church, so making friendships that would lift him out of himself. The young people welcomed him and took him along to the Saturday afternoon tennis club. Unfortunately he was hopeless at tennis and this only made things worse than ever.

His depression grew so great that one day he told me he was seriously tempted to commit suicide. A divided home was contributing to his sense of insecurity and depression. He described his habit of lying in bed for hours worrying about his inferiority, or fuming with rage about people who had, in his opinion, slighted him or failed to do what he thought they should. Even after a good night's sleep he would wake early in the morning and then just lie there allowing negative and destructive thoughts to flood his mind. He was consuming his spiritual, mental and physical energies before he ever began the day's work. No wonder he was constantly tired and depressed. Now he had obviously reached a crisis.

With the help of his psychiatrist and the usual spiritual approach we managed to get him through that bad patch, but he was still in a serious state until one day we discovered he had a flair for painting. We prevailed on him to do one or two placards for church organizations. These impressed a business man in the congregation who gave him a permanent position. In a time he became one of the happiest and most useful members of the church. He had learned to accept his limitations and to develop the talents God had given him. His story had a happy ending because he turned to God for the solution of his problem. Until he did so, however, he was in danger of real disaster because his personality was being torn by two most destructive forces, feelings of inferiority and feelings of irritation. In this chapter I am concerned with the answer provided by the Christian faith to both these problems.

1

Feelings of inferiority.—One of the problems which makes life so interesting is whether it is wiser to battle with our deficiencies and overcome them, thus turning liabilities into assets, or to ignore them as far as possible and concentrate on developing the talents God has given us. We all admire the man who begins life with unfair handicaps and who still wins the victory. We like to hear of people who have actually made capital out of a handicap. In the third chapter of the Book of Judges there is a bloodthirsty story which illustrates this point. The children of Israel had been enslaved for eighteen years by Eglon, the obese and cruel king of Moab. They cried out for a deliverer and one appeared from a most unexpected quarter, Ehud, the son of Gera who was left-handed. Today we worry little about such things. Indeed it is so common that on an average I would say that in one out of five weddings I conduct, at least one signature is made by a left-handed person. But in the old days such people were shunned and even persecuted as being allied to the powers of evil. No wonder many of them became embittered against society and developed malevolent tendencies. But not Ehud. Responding to the national yearning for a deliverer, he risked his life to set the people free and used his handicap to achieve his object. Taking a present to their enemy he sought a private audience with him in a summer house. Eglon was naturally suspicious and looked for any sign of a weapon where it would normally be carried, on a man's left side. Seeing none he sent his men away. As soon as they were alone Ehud with his left hand seized a dagger which he had hidden on his right side and plunged it into Eglon. Then bolting the door he made his escape before the king's retainers realized there was anything wrong. Emboldened by his success Ehud summoned the people to battle. Gladly now they followed the left-handed leader and drove the invader out of their country. So the land had peace for another eighty years.

By all means let us battle with our handicaps and if possible use them to achieve great things. But let us be on our guard lest we give too much time and energy to this and thereby neglect the more important responsibility of using our positive qualities in the service of God. During my university days I deliberately chose one particular subject because I was weak in it. It annoyed me to think it could baffle me and I was determined to conquer it with the help of the outstanding professor we had at the time. I was not at all displeased with the final result, but looking back now I realize that it cost me a tremendous amount of really difficult work which was always a drudgery. Furthermore, apart from the personal satisfaction I gained from the final class-list, I doubt whether all that work made much real contribution to my later ministry. In those days I shared a study for a short time with a friend who had not been regarded as outstanding in the academic side at school. His trouble had been that he was weak in mathematics and certain other compulsory subjects. Now at the university he left all these behind him and concentrated on the subjects he liked. He finished up with brilliant honors.

My advice to students now is this, life is too short to worry about your weak subjects unless they are absolutely essential to your chosen career. Concentrate on your strong subjects. God has put us into this world to serve our fellow men and he has selected for us special talents for that purpose. He expects us to develop and use those talents and not to be jealous of others because of the talents which they possess and which we do not.

There is a prayer of Professor John Baillie's which has often helped me, "It is Thou, O hidden One, who dost appoint my lot and determine the bounds of my habitation. It is Thou who has put power into my hand to do one work and withheld the skill to do another."

"My peace I give unto you," said Jesus, and he does give it to those who learn to accept their limitations. Many years ago a young Scottish missionary in South Africa named Andrew Murray wooed and won a sixteen-year-old Huguenot girl. They had seventeen children of whom twelve survived. Some years ago this family could count 304 descendants. Of these 42 had become ministers of the gospel with several others training for the same calling. At least three members of the family entered politics and almost without exception the whole Murray clan has been a blessing to the Union of South Africa. When asked what was the secret of the family strength they generally pointed back to old Grandmother Murray, the Huguenot girl of other days. Somebody once asked the old lady how she managed to bring up such a wonderful family and she replied, "I'm sure I don't know. I didn't do anything." She was modest about it, but her children and grandchildren knew the answer. Their great anchor had been her godly serenity. She was always content to be where her Heavenly Father wanted her to be. She spent many hours in communion with him and somehow managed to transmit his spirit to those whom she loved. She could not have done it had she developed a rebellious spirit after losing five children, or had she made a habit of complaining that she had been deprived of a "good time" when she assumed the responsibilities of a housewife and a mother at such an early age. No, she gladly accepted the limitations that were hers, praised God for all her many other blessings and became a woman who left a mark on history.

To me one of the most striking of the printed sermons of Peter Marshall is the one entitled *Disciples in Clay*.[1] He considered what would have happened had there been an examining board to choose the disciples. Peter would have appeared before them smelling of fish, an uncouth person—not at all refined, or cultured or educated. He was blustering, blundering, clumsy, impulsive. They would not have passed Peter. James and John would have appeared before such a board as boastful and impatient, most unsuitable people. Nathaniel was lazy. Thomas a cynic, Matthew had sold his soul for money. So Peter Marshall took every one of the disciples and considered their limitations. Not one of them was suitable for the high task to which Jesus was calling them. But Jesus did not look at their limitations or their past failures. He saw only their possibilities. He evoked in them qualities and talents they did not know they possessed. Any one of them could have developed a fierce inferiority complex. But Jesus took each man, gave him a new vision of what life could be and showed him what he could do in the mightiest enterprise ever set before men. Then as each found faith in him and devoted his life to him, a new power was released in his personality. Along with that power came a great new sense of inner peace. The peace which Christ offers us is not release from activity, but the peace which comes from finding our true purpose in life. An aircraft mechanic will tell you that when an engine is working perfectly it sings. So it is with your soul and mine. When we are wholly engaged in the work to which he calls us then, and only then, do we really understand what he meant when he said, "My peace I give unto you."

[1]*Mr. Jones, Meet the Master*, London, Peter Davies, 1954 (pp. 39–52).

Feelings of irritation. —The other force which is so destructive to mental peace and spiritual serenity is persistent irritation. We all have a combative instinct. Without it few would have survived in the cave-man era. In the normal circumstances of civilized existence we have more combativeness than we need and because of social convention we have to suppress a considerable amount of our aggression. One of the reasons why I like golf so much is the opportunity it gives to work off such feelings by hitting a ball very hard.

The suppression of aggressiveness does strange things to some people. In 1951 I had the privilege, along with the Rev. Dr. Irving Benson of Wesley Church, Melbourne, of organizing a preaching and lecturing mission in Australia for Dr. Leslie Weatherhead at that time still minister of the City Temple, London. Throughout the preliminary negotiations, I noticed that Dr. Weatherhead signed all his letters in green ink, a point which added greater interest to the story told in his book *Psychology in the Service of the Soul.*[1]

Dr. Weatherhead had given a lecture in Liverpool in the course of which he stated that when we forget the names of people it may be because unconsciously we dislike them. Later the organizer of the meeting who had never met Dr. Weatherhead before and, therefore, had no reason for either liking or disliking him, challenged the statement on the grounds that twice that evening he had forgotten his name. Weatherhead questioned him more closely and said, "Whom do you dislike most in the world?" At once the man said, "My boss." "Why do you dislike him?" asked Weatherhead. "Because when he has a complaint to make, instead of making it to me directly he sends me a typewritten letter signed in ridiculous green ink." Weatherhead then reminded him that in their correspondence about the meeting his own letters had been signed in the same way. The organizer had been unconsciously transferring his antipathy to Weatherhead.

[1] Epworth Press.

The same influence was at work in the famous incident concerning "Rabbi" Duncan, the noted Professor of Hebrew in Scotland of other days. Like many academic people Duncan detested social gatherings. One evening his wife appeared dressed all ready to go to such an engagement and admonished him that he had not changed into his good suit for the occasion. He had forgotten all about it and hurried upstairs to rectify matters. As he was a long time returning, his wife went up to investigate and found him in bed. His mind had wandered off on to his familiar academic subjects as he began to disrobe and from force of habit he finished up in his pajamas instead of his good suit.

Sometimes feelings of irritation have more serious effects, especially when the irritation exists between husband and wife. We all have this combative instinct, this fighting spirit which has to express itself in some way. It is sometimes said of a poor henpecked little fellow who never answers back his wife and who is pushed around at the office all day that there is no fight in him. In point of fact that is where it all is. It is pushed down inside, kept in. That is why he is moody and unhappy. Consequently some psychologists assert that husbands and wives who quarrel occasionally are more healthily adjusted than couples who do not. If they do not express their irritation, they are in danger of building up more and more tension inside with the danger of a volcanic eruption at some future date. Either that or it will produce physical troubles like ulcers, some forms of asthma, colitis, blood pressure or bilious attacks. It would be wrong, however, to jump to the conclusion that if you haven't had a quarrel with your wife lately you are headed for a gastric ulcer! Here as in all our human problems Jesus Christ has the answer. To married couples as to individuals He says, "My peace I give unto you." He leads husbands and wives to sublimate their combative instinct. Instead of directing it at one another they learn to combine the forces within them in constructive ways for the well-being of the family and the building of the Kingdom of God.

The greatest example I can think of in regard to the sublimation of the combative instinct is the story of the Apostle Paul. Here was a man who loved a fight. He was never out of them. Both before and after his conversion he was always mixed up in some kind of battle, but what a difference it made when he allowed Christ to take charge of his life!

When we first meet Paul he is present at the fight between Stephen and the enemies of the Christian faith. Paul was helping those who threw the stones at Stephen. Next we find him "breathing out threatenings and slaughter against the disciples of the Lord," obtaining a commission to go to distant Damascus to root them out there. Surely he could have left them in peace so far away, but not Paul. His combative instinct was roused. His fighting spirit was up and he had to go. There was no fiercer enemy of Christ than he.

On the road to Damascus, Paul came to the fight of his life. It was with an antagonist he could neither see nor touch, but it was the most terrific fight he ever fought. It completely changed his life and the course of human history. He heard a voice saying, "It is hard for thee to kick against the pricks." In those days beasts of burden were driven with long goads which had a sharp prick on the end. If an animal was refractory the sharp point would be jabbed into its rump. A fighting animal would kick against the pricks only to get itself hurt more and more. Paul now realized that in fighting Jesus Christ, he himself was the one who was getting hurt. At last he yielded to his conqueror and said, "Lord, what wouldst Thou have me to do?"

It was then that Christ took Paul's combative instinct, his fighting spirit and directed it into an entirely new channel. It was no use Paul pretending he did not have it, no use trying to suppress it into his unconscious mind. To use it as he had been using it was doing immense harm to others as to himself. Now he was led to see how he could turn its force into building the Kingdom of God. The second half of the Book of Acts is the story of how Paul sublimated his combative instinct. In the 15th chapter we find him using it in the council of the church at Jerusalem to win the great battle for the gentiles. Then we see him at Philippi battling with vested interests for the soul of a fortune-telling girl. In city after city we see him arguing with his fellow Jews in the synagogues. When Jews and gentiles combined to stone him, or flog him out of one city, he calmly went to the next city and started the same kind of fight all over again. Not content with that he would set off on another missionary journey to revisit exactly the same towns to take up the fight where he had left off. Danger seemed to fascinate him. At one stage it became apparent that quite the most dangerous place for Paul to appear in would be Jerusalem. From then on nothing would do but for Paul to go back there, though at every stopping place on the way friends pleaded with him in tears not to go on. But he went, and in no time there was a crowd yelling for his blood. So Paul was arrested yet again and sent to Caesarea where he argued with the Jewish King and Queen and the Roman Governor. What a fighter he was! At the end, he reviewed his life and remembered all these things. But he had no regrets. He wrote to his friend Timothy saying, "I have fought a good fight." That is the point isn't it? Life is a battle whether we want it that way or not. If we are to stand loyally for Christ, it will be all the more of a battle. But Christ can touch that combative instinct, that fighting spirit of ours and make it sublime. By his grace we can fight the good fight.

Let us remember these things when we are moved by feelings of irritation. Usually it is our own fighting spirit seeking an outlet. Often these feelings are prompted by the combative instinct in somebody else. Perhaps you are a Sunday school teacher and you have a boy in your class who is a little tiger. If you can bring him under the influence of Jesus Christ, he might become another Apostle Paul. Perhaps you serve on some committee in which there is a problem member always causing trouble. Pray for that member that Christ may use his combative instinct for constructive ends. Wonderful results can follow. If this instinct is causing trouble among your friends or within your family circle, do remember that it is a God-given force which has found the wrong expression. There is one who has said "My peace I give unto you." The Bible records, "He knew what was in men." No one knows more about us than Jesus and when each one of us comes, as Paul did on the road to Damascus to say, "Lord what wilt Thou have me to do?" then we will find how to direct our fighting spirit not into some paltry and selfish battle, but into the real battle, the battle for the Kingdom of God. And the strange thing is that when we get into that battle with all our heart and mind and soul, then we discover his peace, the peace of God which passeth all understanding.

Once again we find acceptance the key to serenity. We must learn to accept ourselves as God made us and to develop the talents he has entrusted to us without pining for those we do not possess. We must learn to accept our combative instinct and with his help direct it into constructive and satisfying channels. Then power will flow through us.

Chapter Five

ACCEPTING PEOPLE

A young lady, who later became well-known to me, once wrote me a letter describing how she had discovered serenity by changing her attitude towards difficult people. Her story began in a small country town. At the time she was a school-teacher, and she was far from happy. In her opinion the principal was a most difficult person and the children "got on her nerves." She was a long way from home with the result that the weekends were even harder to bear than ordinary days. To her it was a dead kind of town. There was nothing to do but go on studying and working. She had not attended church for years, and it did not occur to her that, if nothing else, worship would at least break this weary routine which threatened to drive her out of her mind.

Her one relaxation was listening to the radio, but one Sunday night owing to freak atmospheric conditions she could pick up none of the usual stations. So she happened to tune in one of my radio broadcasts and came to know the serenity prayer:—

"God grant me serenity to accept the things I cannot change, courage to change things I can and wisdom to know the difference."

This prayer stood her in good stead later, but unfortunately it did not come to her in time to prevent the breakdown which had been threatening. The incessant round of work and her obsession with it, together with irritation at the children and the principal brought about a collapse which compelled her to resign her position.

After prolonged treatment her doctor pronounced her fit to take another appointment. Some readers may be able to appreciate her feelings as she travelled in the train to her new school. Would her nerves stand the strain? Would the new principal be as difficult as the last? Would she be able to control the children? She was rapidly working herself into a serious state, when she remembered the serenity prayer. She kept repeating it, applying it in particular to the people whom she was yet to meet. The result was not only a sense of calm, but a feeling of actual enthusiasm as she looked forward to her new appointment. Instead of going into her interview with the principal in a state of tension, filled with resentment and antagonism, to tell him as she had done on similar occasions in the past that she did not like the school or her appointment to it, she went in willing to co-operate and to seek the best in the situation. This new attitude enabled her to look for the best in the principal and the children also. When we seek the best we usually find it. So it was that by changing her mental attitude she changed the whole situation for herself and for many others. I do not say that all difficulties magically disappeared, but this experience so strengthened her faith that some time later she was able to cope with a family tragedy and still rise triumphant. Today she is a well-adjusted personality and a most useful member of the community.

Many people have learned the art of finding serenity by accepting the things they cannot change. When we accept things in the mind the emotions are no longer in conflict. This tumult is the cause of much of our exhaustion. What I particularly want to emphasize now is the Christian duty of accepting not only things, but people we cannot change. Perhaps you are a wife whose husband gets on your nerves, or a business man with a problem employee, or a parent with a wayward child, or a middle-aged person with an elderly and petulant parent, or an employee with somebody over you who makes life difficult. I doubt if there is anybody whose life is not hindered, indeed, darkened, by some relative or some associate in business. If it is impossible to change them, we only wear ourselves out by worrying. Rather let us pray, "God grant me serenity to accept the people I cannot change, courage to change those I can, and wisdom to know the difference." There are solid New Testament grounds for adopting this kind of attitude. Consider four great words which were constantly on the lips of Jesus Christ and his apostles.

1

Forbearance.—The Apostle Paul wrote in Colossians 3:13, "Forbearing one another and forgiving one another, if any man hath a quarrel against any: even as Christ forgave you, so also do ye." J. B. Phillips translates that, "Accept life, and be patient and tolerant with one another, always ready to forgive if you have a difference with any one. Forgive as freely as Christ has forgiven you."

I think of a wife who was troubled because her marriage appeared to be breaking up. A coldness had developed between her husband and herself. He kept doing things which irritated her. Frequently she became filled with fury because he kept on doing them though he knew that she didn't like it. Daily the tension increased until she felt she wanted to scream. As he went off to work each morning she would go to her room and cry her heart out.

She was brooding upon her problem as usual one day when she happened to pick up a religious magazine. It gave her an entirely new slant on things. She realized that she had developed a hopelessly negative attitude towards her husband, seeing all his faults and blinding herself to his many virtues. She reminded herself that, whereas, many other women had heartaches because their husbands were not faithful to them, or were problem drinkers, he at least was showing fidelity and lived a sober life. She now turned to God for help and as she did so she realized that much of the fault was in herself. She had developed this negative attitude toward her husband because she had forgotten her marriage vows to take him for better, for worse. Remembering that the first years of their marriage had been happy enough she decided there must have been something enduring and that somehow their marriage could be rebuilt. As she switched to this new attitude and looked for the good in her husband and not the bad, he responded to it and their old happiness returned. Some days she slipped into the old habit of fault-finding and she soon found that it produced a reaction in her husband which revived all the old tension.

As I often remind couples when I marry them, to me there is nothing more wonderful than that anyone should take the one life they have and all that they are and give it to another for better, for worse till death. If you are constantly grateful to one another and to God for this wonderful gift, the spirit of gratitude enriches and strengthens your marriage all down through the years. If it does nothing else, it keeps your mind positive. It certainly helps to preserve the serenity to accept your mate as he or she is.

2

Forgiveness.—A second great New Testament word which we must all lay to heart if we are to solve the problems of difficult personal relationships is the word "forgiveness." Why is it that most of us find it so terribly hard to forgive, even when it must be obvious that by refusing to forgive we are the ones who suffer most? Peter said to Jesus, "Lord, how oft shall my brother sin against me and I forgive him? Till seven times?" Knowing something of Peter's temperament in those days we can well imagine him feeling mighty big-hearted when he said, "Till seven times?" He lived in a place and at a time when men regarded the taking of vengeance as a sacred duty. But Jesus said, "I say not unto thee, Until seven times: but Until seventy times seven." If you find it difficult to accept that difficult person in your life, remember the Christian duty to forgive unto seventy times seven.

3

Faith.—The third word which I take from the New Testament to support my contention that we must learn to accept people is the word "faith." We must believe in people as Jesus did. He showed faith in the most hopeless charac-ters. He believed in those who were called "publicans and sinners." If we described them as "stand-over men and down-and-outs," it would probably conjure up a more exact picture of the kind of people with whom he chose to asso-ciate. Yet he did associate with them because he knew there was still good that could be called forth. He believed in rough, hard-swearing half-educated fishermen like Peter, James and John and made them the foundation of his church. He believed in people who seemed to be incurably selfish like Zaccheus and Matthew. He believed in people whose lives and whose mental health had been wrecked by lust, people like Mary of Magdala and the woman taken in sin. To such people he said, "Neither do I condemn you, go and sin no more." If he could accept people like that, surely you and I can accept people who sin against us!

More than that, if he believed that they could still do great things with their lives, as they did when inspired by him, surely we can look for the buried treasure in the problem people we have to deal with and enter into the great Christian adventure of bringing forth that treasure. It probably only needs a little encouragement, a little faith, forbearance and forgiveness to produce wonderful results.

Onesimus was a no-good slave. He had stolen from his master and run away. Knowing his life was forfeit if he were caught, he was a desperate man. So in due course he came to Rome hoping to hide himself in the great city. There he met the Apostle Paul and heard for the first time the story of Jesus Christ. He found people who treated him with affection and respect in place of the hatred and contempt which he had known most of his life. They showed faith in him and he responded. As he talked over his problem with Paul they decided the only solution was for Onesimus to go back to his master, Philemon, and throw himself on his mercy. Naturally Onesimus had qualms about it. It was a fearful risk to take. If Philemon did not forgive, Onesimus would not be long for this world. But how could he accept the Christian life and go on living with his guilty conscience? It is extraordinary the number of people who come to ministers in these days and confess sins which not another soul knows anything about, or could know anything about. Yet they have to get it off their conscience and until they do all their life is darkened. Well, so it was with Onesimus. To strengthen his case and give him courage Paul wrote a letter for him to Philemon. In this letter Paul made play upon the name Onesimus which means "Useful." Paul knows full well how useless Philemon must have regarded him. No doubt Philemon often told him he was no use. So he knocked the heart out of the man and first gave him ideas of running away. But now listen to what Paul writes (as J. B. Phillips translates it), "Oh, I know you have found him pretty useless in the past but he is going to be useful now, to both of us." There is nothing that restores a man's self-respect more than the assurance that he is important to somebody. Knowing how Paul felt about him, Onesimus had the courage to begin a new life. There must have been a happy ending to the story, otherwise we would hardly have had the Epistle to Philemon preserved as a book in the New Testament to this day. That is what faith in one problem child accomplished.

Love.—The fourth and greatest word from the New Testament is the word "love." Without this, as Paul emphasized, we are just a lot of noise. With it anything is possible. In the section on forbearance I quoted a verse from Colossians. There is a similar verse in the fourth chapter of Ephesians containing these words, "Forbearing one another in love." Phillips gives that a nice twist by translating it, "Making allowances for each other because you love each other." I thought of that one day as I watched a father and mother on a ferry trip across a harbor. Their small boy had one of those objectionable little tin beetles which make a loud clicking noise when you squeeze it. For a long time the child clicked this thing in their ears. Yet they showed no impatience with him. Not content with that, the child pulled out a small trumpet and proceeded to blast the air with a most unmusical series of noises. Still his parents were undisturbed, and they remained undisturbed while he consumed a sticky candy and then proceeded to crawl all over them. They affectionately cleaned him up and continued to play with him. To me it was a wonderful illustration of "making allowances for each other because you love each other." If only we could carry something of the same spirit into our normal human relationships there would be much more tolerance in the world.

It can be done when we are prepared to allow the spirit of Christ to control our lives. Jesus, we are told, loved the rich young ruler even when he was still putting his money before the things which really matter. Everything Jesus did was motivated by his own divine love. He was entirely free from the corroding acid of hatred for human beings, however evil they were.

Booker T. Washington, the black scientist and Christian, who was frequently insulted and ill-treated by prejudiced white people, once remarked, "I will not let any man reduce my soul to the level of hatred." If we train ourselves to accept people, whatever they do, because they are all children of

God and beloved by him, then we cleanse ourselves of hatred and bring the great blessing of love to them and to ourselves. There is no greater curse than hatred and no greater blessing than love.

Once in Scotland I had the privilege of spending a night as a guest in the home of Professor George Duncan of St. Andrews. For that reason I was particularly interested in a tribute to him written by Earl Haig, the famous Commander-in-Chief during the First World War. In those days Duncan was a chaplain, scarcely out of the university and a youth about half the age of the great military leader. Haig did not despise his youth. He believed in him and treated him with respect as a dedicated man of God. Haig brought the best out of the young chaplain. After the Armistice he wrote a letter to Duncan saying, "It was very difficult to keep going all through the time of the long war; and I am frequently asked how I managed to do it. Well, I can truly say that you were a great help to me in putting things into proper perspective on Sundays."

We bring the best out of people when we treat them with forbearance, forgiveness, faith and love.

Chapter Six

ACCEPTING SECOND PLACE

FROM the casebook of a psychiatrist I take the story of Barbara. Before she was a year old both her parents died, and she spent the next four years being bundled from one group of relatives to another, unloved and unwanted. In her fifth year she was finally adopted by a distant cousin, a maiden lady named Cousin Clara. Now Barbara received the love for which she was starved, but she was so frightened of losing it that she hastened to comply with every slightest whim on the part of Cousin Clara.

Anxious that Barbara should be admired and popular, Cousin Clara urged her to be kind and polite to all her little playmates, giving in to them in everything even though they tore her hair-ribbons, smashed her dolls and walked off with her picture books. It became such a habit with Barbara that years later she still submitted while other women pushed her around, borrowed her clothes, and absconded with her boy-friends. Barbara went on meekly playing second-fiddle, but deep down suppressed rage was producing fits of awful depression which frightened her.

In the same way Cousin Clara unintentionally was responsible for something of a guilt complex in Barbara. On several occasions she caught Barbara preening herself in front of a mirror and each time Barbara received a severe lecture on the sin of vanity. When she grew up, not only was she unable to make the most of her personal appearance, but she actually had feelings of guilt whenever she saw a mirror or heard the word "cosmetics." On top of that Cousin Clara frequently reminded Barbara that her father had died a drunkard and there was a good deal of work to be done on Barbara's character to prevent her taking after her father. Barbara began to feel responsible for her father's imperfections as well as her own. It is a great pity that Cousin Clara could not have adopted a more positive and loving attitude. She might have pointed out to the sensitive child that her father had many excellent qualities in spite of his "disease." Barbara's rich imagination and ability in the English class were inherited in no small measure from her father. Even though she topped the class she gained little pleasure from it because Cousin Clara was determined she should not become conceited about it. Barbara actually felt guilty because she had done well.

Leaving school Barbara obtained a position in an advertising firm. While she was left in her little cubby-hole to write copy, she was content. She became so useful to the firm that they thought of promoting her. This would mean dealing with other people and Barbara panicked. In spite of herself she picked a quarrel with the very executive who was trying to help her. Eventually she married a man much older than herself with a dominating disposition. Her attitude of unnatural compliance with its thinly-veiled resentment, provoked his more intense domination until she could endure it no longer and fled with only the clothes on her back. Eventually she was divorced for desertion.

At this point in her misery Barbara found her way to a psychiatrist who probed her early history and explained the nature of her "compulsive compliant neurosis," as he called it. The immediate result of this treatment was to make Barbara such an aggressive woman that a whole set of new problems developed. The psychiatrist assures us that eventually the pendulum returned to a normal position and Barbara was able to find adjustment of personality.

I have quoted that story as an illustration of the misery brought into human lives by excessive domination on the one hand by such people as Cousin Clara and the husband, and, on the other, by the resentment that people feel when they are the victims of such domination and have not yet found the Christian answer to the problem. The difficult people we considered in the previous chapter are so often difficult because they must have their own way regardless of the feelings of others. A wife frets away her serenity and health because her husband is domineering; a husband burns up his spiritual resources because he is yoked with a wife who must have the last say in everything; there are quarrels among children when one insists on "bossing" the others. The same spirit produces tension in offices, factories, social groups, sporting teams and—let it be admitted—even in churches. If only there were some means of enabling people to be happy in second place, while modifying the selfishness which produces tyrants, what a different world it would be! In this chapter I am mainly concerned with the first problem, how can we learn to accept second place and be happy in it without surrendering anything that is worthwhile? The great thing about Christianity is that it teaches people to play second-fiddle and to be free of resentment and tension caused by jealousy, not by breaking the spirit, but by strengthening it. Those who discover the true nature of Christian meekness discover a pearl of great price.

1

Christian meekness is a serene spirit based on a secure faith in God.—The kind of meekness shown by Barbara is a weak spirit which sooner or later leads to disaster. It springs from unworthy motives. When Jesus said, "Blessed are the meek for they shall inherit the earth," he certainly did not mean that kind of attitude, nor did he exhibit it in himself. There was no cringing compliance about him. His meekness was the meekness of great power which of itself chooses to be gentle. It is the meekness of a personality filled with passion which yet strictly controls and disciplines that passion. The French translate this text, "Blessed are the debonair." The ideal of a true gentleman comes very near to it, the man who is gracious, self-controlled, polite, temperate and above all considerate of others. There is nothing weak about Christian meekness. It is robust, mainly, Christlike. We need never be ashamed of showing deference and consideration to others. That is how Christ chose to be. That is how he calls us to live.

Without a strong faith in the love and power of God it is difficult to maintain that attitude toward our fellow human beings. If Barbara had realized from the beginning how important she was to God and that she could never lose his love, she would not have been so terrified by the thought of losing the love of Cousin Clara or the regard of her play-mates. Perhaps it is difficult for a child to attain that faith, but it is necessary for adults to grow into it if they are to escape the torment of those whose whole lives are deter-mined by "what will people think?" or the particular kind of torment we are considering in this chapter expressed by the complaint, "Why do I always have to give in?"

A right attitude to God and a right relationship with him give us that inner serenity and sense of security which set us free from tension and thereby enable us to enter into a right, and therefore a happier, relationship with those round about us. Sooner or later we have to accept the idea that we all play second-fiddle to God. He rules the universe. We do not. Yet how many people persist in adopting the attitude that if there is a God, he exists to play second-fiddle to them? That attitude lies behind the expression we hear so often, "God doesn't answer my prayers." If they could see the truth more clearly and were honest about it they would say, "God refuses to play second-fiddle to me."

Once we see the truth and come into a right relationship

with God then we rejoice to play second-fiddle to him and we can hardly do that without playing second-fiddle to our fellow men and women. Nevertheless, if we are prepared to be used by God, God can do great things through us. There is not a man or woman in the Bible whom we honor today who did not begin where Moses began, or Isaiah, Jeremiah, Peter, Paul or a hundred others. They began at the point of meekness before God saying, "Who am I that I should go? Nevertheless, here am I Lord, send me." That is the kind of meekness which inherits the earth.

There is another way in which the right relationship with God produces serenity. Barbara might have gone through life fairly comfortably had it not been for the deep suppressed rages which destroyed her peace and provoked irrational quarrels at most unfortunate times. It is not so much what happens *to* us as what happens *in* us that is important. It is our reaction that does the harm. Those who learn to accept what comes to them as being God's will for them are set free from the boiling rage and resentment which corrode the soul and destroy peace of mind.

Some years ago a fellow-student had set his heart on winning a Rhodes Scholarship to Oxford. He had worked for years with that one goal in view and in the end just missed out. At first he was greatly discouraged and felt inclined to give up the struggle altogether. Fortunately he was a man of faith and believed that God never shuts one door without opening another. He came to see that God had some plan for him which did not include the Rhodes Scholarship. Several years later he was awarded an entirely different scholarship. He would certainly not have been considered had it not been for all the work he had put in earlier. Nor would he have been considered had he given up the struggle in disgust. But now this scholarship proved far more valuable for his life's work and his ultimate service to the community than the Rhodes Scholarship would have done in his case. Meekness before God is the gateway through which we pass to inherit the earth.

Christian meekness springs from an entirely new attitude toward our fellow men.—In the natural world some people are meek, like Barbara, because of fear or from policy or because of some other unworthy motive. The Christian is meek because of love and that is the only meekness which is constructive both for ourselves and others. Without such faith we look on other people as rivals for what we want and we can't bear to see them going ahead of us. But when we are bound to one another in the bonds of Christian love and are all seeking first the Kingdom of God, then we are enabled to rejoice that somebody with greater qualifications than our own is able to take the leadership. Not only that, but we rejoice to help them and serve them in our secondary position for the sake of the cause which is so much greater than any of us. Think of some of the outstanding second-fiddles of history. Where would Moses have been without Aaron, or Paul without Barnabas or Silas? Where would Moody have been without Sankey, or Chapman without Alexander, Helen Keller without Miss Sullivan or Billy Graham without Cliff Barrows, or Norman Vincent Peale without his wife Ruth? Behind a thousand other great men there is a loyal and loving wife who does not mind playing second-fiddle to the man in her life. So because of her he is able to achieve great things. Such a wife shares in the ultimate joy and glory.

Before we turn to consider in more detail the rewards of Christian meekness, let us note one aspect of it which is seen very clearly in the case of Jesus himself. His meekness would endure all kind of personal insult, but it would not endure insults to other people. Jesus controlled his anger even when his enemies spat in his face, but how that same anger blazed forth when he thought of people offending little children or when he saw them desecrating the temple of God! Anger controlled in regard to personal insults is all the more violent when it blazes forth against wrong in other directions.

Christian meekness brings its own wonderful rewards.—Jesus promised that the meek would inherit the earth. As one commentator put it, "Meekness is a world-conquering principle." I have developed this theme in Chapter 3 of my earlier book *Happiness is a Habit* and will not enlarge on it here. However, let me refer briefly to two or three ways in which the meek do inherit the earth.

For one thing, being mindful of our dependence upon God, we learn to enjoy his universe. Every flower, every tree, every sunset, every cup of cold water is a new gift from our Heavenly Father. We can enjoy these things even more than Traddles in *David Copperfield* who would wander with his wife through the great London emporiums enjoying all the wonderful displays though they never bought anything. It is a great thing to acquire the capacity to enjoy without having to possess in an economic sense. The meek inherit the earth in this way.

Again the meek are truly adjusted to God's universe and, therefore, benefit most from it. The scientist must submit to the physical laws of the universe before he can do anything with them or produce any great invention. If he decides, for instance, that the operation of the law of gravity is inconvenient for his purposes and proceeds as though it did not exist, he gets nowhere except to disaster. Yet how many people treat the spiritual laws of God with the same kind of stupidity because of the spirit which is the opposite of meekness—human pride and selfishness. One spiritual law which thousands persist in ignoring is the commandment which bids us rest on the Sabbath day. Sooner or later those who defy this commandment pay the price in spiritual disorientation. As the scientist masters life by submitting to the laws of nature, so does the believer master life by submitting to spiritual laws. The meek, in the sense of the obedient, inherit the earth.

Finally the meek inherit the earth by serving. Servants become the real rulers of their masters by becoming indispensable. So Jesus, the Master of every situation, was never more Master of mankind than when He submitted to the cross. "I, if I be lifted up," he said, "will draw all men unto me." Tyrants and dictators who attain a temporary notoriety for their capacity to get their own way march ultimately to destruction. The loving and meek Christ is slowly but surely inheriting the earth. Let us lay to heart the familiar words of Napoleon:—"Alexander Caesar, Charlemagne and I myself have founded empires; but upon what do these creations of our genius depend? Upon force. Jesus alone founded his empire upon love; and to this very day millions would die for him."

Chapter Seven

ACCEPTING LIBERTY

TOO many people lack serenity because they have not found the liberty of spirit offered by Christianity. They feel frustrated, chained to an unsatisfactory existence, "cabin'd, cribbed, confined, bound in" as Shakespeare put it. They long for the wings of a dove, then would fly away and be at rest, not realizing that until they find spiritual freedom they would be still a captive however far they flew. We can't escape from ourselves, and it is in our own souls that the battle is won or lost.

Liberty to the Christian believer comes first of all to those who are prepared to accept truth, especially the truth as it is in Him. "You will know the truth and the truth will set you free," said Jesus referring to his own teaching (John 8:32 N.E.B.).

Few things are more enslaving than ignorance. Dr. Norman Maclean of St. Cuthbert's, Edinburgh, was born on the island of Skye off the west coast of Scotland. It is an island of rare and rugged beauty and we love to sing of its mountains, the far Coolins and their "calling." But it is a poverty-stricken island, and the people who live there have a constant physical battle against the elements to eke out a living. Young Norman Maclean's mother believed that the boy had something in him and that one day he would do great things in the world. She realized that he would need a better education than he could achieve on the island if that dream were to come true. She talked it over with her husband in their little thatched cottage one night, but he was not responsive. He was already spending all the money he could possibly afford to educate their elder boy. Besides, in his opinion, young Norman was *gorach*—a Gaelic word meaning half-witted. He based this on Norman's conviction that 9 times 9 was 85 and not 81 as was plainly stated on the back of their Shorter Catechism. Undiscouraged the mother went on believing in the boy, praying that a miracle would happen to give him his chance. One day it did. A visiting minister who had control of a certain scholarship, impressed with the boy's possibilities, invited him to write an essay. In due course on a never-to-be-forgotten day a letter arrived saying that the essay was of such quality that the scholarship had been awarded to Norman Maclean. It was valued at only $75 a year, but it was a fortune to this poverty-stricken family, and it opened the door to Norman's higher education. The volume of his autobiography which is devoted to this portion of his life is entitled *Set Free* and the particular chapter is called *Deliverance*.

In one sense Norman Maclean had entered a new kind of slavery. While his comrades back in Skye were free to fish and climb mountains or go where they liked, he was in Inverness tied down to his studies bound to "scorn delights and live laborious days." Yet, through that discipline, in due course there was released all the latent power of his great personality to his own enrichment and the blessing of many thousands. If the acquisition of some knowledge set free the powers that were in Norman Maclean, how much more will the truth about God as it is in Christ Jesus set free the possibilities in all of us. "I am the way, the truth and the life," said Jesus. Again He said, "This is life eternal that they may know thee the only true God and Jesus Christ whom thou hast sent" (John 17:3). It has been proved again and again that when a man comes face to face with the truth as it is in Jesus, when he accepts that truth in his mind, when he "accepts" Jesus Christ in faith, then a new spirit and a new power, bringing new life, enter into him. "Where the spirit of our Lord is, there is liberty" (2 Corinthians 3:17). Phillips translates it, "wherever the Spirit of the Lord is, men's souls are set free."

1

Consider now what happens when the spirit of the Lord enters a believer to set him free from the power of sin. We commonly think of liberty as release from all restriction so that we may do what we like. But the man who only does what he likes is a slave to his own desires. Whence do they come? Usually from the baser side of his nature. No man is more to be pitied than the man who is a slave to his instincts, a slave to self.

Jesus taught us to deny self, but not to despise ourselves. Indeed he lifted humanity to a new dignity, assuring us that each one of us is precious in the sight of God, even as the smallest sparrow. He urged us to develop our talents and hence our personalities in the service of God and his kingdom. His Apostle Paul commanded us to present our bodies a living (not a dead) sacrifice, holy, acceptable unto God. The paradox is that as we deny self we enter into a fuller development of personality.

Take friendship. If you are selfish about your friendships, only cultivating friends for what you can get out of them for yourself, you won't keep them very long. If you only talk about yourself people soon weary of you. But if you forget self and become interested in them friendship becomes rich and rewarding.

Take enjoyment. The people who set out to have a good time and to spend all their money selfishly may succeed at first, but in due course they become bored and disillusioned. Those who, like children, become absolutely absorbed in the good things of life and the many blessings God pours out upon us in this wonderful universe, forgetting self altogether, suddenly wake up to discover they have been having a wonderful time.

Take achievement. Fritz Kreisler did not become a world-famous violinist by accident. He did it by denying self, practicing boring finger exercises for six long weary hours a day, month after month. It was a form of slavery then, fighting the impulses which called him to more pleasant and more comfortable activities, but it led to a wonderful liberty with the violin in years to come.

Take health. Most people can sleep all right till they start worrying about themselves and whether they will sleep. Then they develop insomnia. The ordinary person enjoys reasonably good health until he starts worrying about it. Our physical life depends to a very great extent on automatic nervous and muscular reflexes. They work quite well until we start thinking about them too much. Then we put them out of order with excessive concern about our health.

Take worry generally. If we could eliminate all our worries about ourselves there would not be very many left. Most people who worry about loved ones are really worrying about themselves. If they had the faith to trust their loved ones to the Lord, the same faith would lift them out of themselves and save them from selfish worry which is so corroding to the soul. Nothing enslaves the spirit more than this kind of worry, but where the spirit of the Lord is, there is liberty from all this.

In speaking of this kind of liberty I am reminded of Psalm 124,

Our soul is escaped as a bird out of the snare of the fowlers: the snare is broken and we are escaped.

Our help is in the name of the Lord, who made heaven and earth.

Scholars tell us that this great psalm was composed in the days of Queen Esther, that beautiful woman who risked her life to deliver her people from destruction at the hands of the wicked Haman. I have no doubt the Hebrew people often sang this psalm as they remembered their deliverance from Egypt and other enemies, "If it had not been for the Lord who was on our side, now may Israel say . . ."

The Huguenots are honored to this day for their incredible endurance in the face of bitter persecution. Most of those who escaped death had to flee from their homes and their native land. One Huguenot family took as its crest a bird escaping from a net, and for its motto these words of Psalm 124, "My soul is escaped, even as a bird out of the snare of the fowler." Earlier the psalm had been turned into a hymn by one of Luther's friends in the great days of the Reformation in Germany and gave untold courage to the hard-pressed Protestants there. Again and again through human history when liberty is threatened by tyrants, those who have the courage to resist are those who have a strong faith in God. The spirit of God is in those who have faith. It is true that where the spirit of the Lord is, there are men set free.

2

God is concerned not only to set us free from evil things, but to lead us into a life of satisfaction, joy and achievement, a life in which all conflicts have been dissolved away and in which we feel free, right and happy.

Once I received a letter from two nurses seeking advice in regard to the problem which confronted them. In one of our great hospitals, surrounded as they were by many worldly people and not a few temptations, they wrote, "we have some difficulty in trying to live practical, Christian lives." I am sure we all sympathize with them. At the same time their letter suggested to me that their conception of a Christian life consisted in not dancing, not smoking, not swearing, not using cosmetics or drinking strong liquor. But does Christianity consist only in *not* doing things? It is something much more positive than that. Jesus set us free from the religion of law. That does not mean that we are free to sin. It means that he gave us a new spirit so that we do not feel the attraction of sinful things. Life with Him is so satisfying that we are just not interested in many things which others feel are necessary if life is to be endured at all. When the spirit of the Lord has given the believer liberty from these things, it makes his life so radiant and rich that others want what we have, even though we may never talk about our religion at all. Norman Maclean paid this tribute to his old minister, the Rev. John Darroch,

"It was his dignity, his kindliness, his lovableness, that first put in my heart the desire to become a minister like him. It is thus the lamp is handed on from generation to generation by voiceless influences."

The best kind of Christians are free from self-conscious concern about the state of their own souls, or whether what they do is right or wrong. They enjoy the "glorious liberty of the children of God."

Two people who illustrate this "glorious liberty" today in my opinion are Billy Graham and his wife Ruth. As I study their ministry together I am reminded of the expression used by the older preachers when they felt a service had gone well. They used to say, "I had great liberty today." In one way they never had less liberty because they were controlled by the Lord, but they were spiritual enough to realize that it was then they were most themselves in the best sense, and most free. Billy Graham tells us that when he gets back from his crusades he makes for his home in a small town in North Carolina. There he has a sound-proof room, and there he studies and restudies his Bible. When the Spirit moves him then he uses three tape recorders and puts down sermon after sermon. I suppose a man with a certain fluency of speech could do that sort of thing, but I don't believe any man could get the results Billy Graham gets unless the Spirit of God gave him the power. I believe he is entirely loyal to that Spirit, entirely obedient insofar as any human being can be. He is still human, and so he still makes mistakes, but according to his consecration so his power comes. Some may regard him as a slave, but I am sure Billy Graham does not think of it as slavery. To him it is such a satisfying life that he wants everybody to share it with him.

It is the same with his wife Ruth. For years she was in a difficult position with several small children to care for and at the same time a world-famous husband who spent nine months of the year travelling from mission to mission. Should she go with her husband or should she stay with the children? She had one simple solution to this problem. She made it a matter of prayer. If the Lord told her to go with her husband she went and refused to fret over the children. If the Lord told her to go back to the children, then she returned because it was the Lord's will and she did not pine for her husband. She was content that he should be about the Lord's work. So she was set free from all those negative emotions which drag down so many people, and so was he. Nothing was wasted because they were both wholly devoted to the Lord and in His service they found perfect freedom.

The late Dr. Harry Ironside of the Moody Tabernacle, Chicago, in his book *Full Assurance* told of a brother minister who had a young man come to say goodbye before sailing for a career in the Far East. The minister felt a concern for the young man's soul and spoke to him about spiritual things, pleading with him to commit himself to Christ before he sailed into this new life which would be full of temptations to a man so far from home. The young man refused saying, "I want to do as I like. I don't see why I should surrender my liberty to Christ or to anybody else." That is the natural, but short-sighted answer of the world. To the man who has a true spiritual experience, the paradox expressed by the blind, but saintly and triumphant George Matheson sums up the truth:

> Make me a captive, Lord,
> And then I shall be free;
> Force me to render up my sword,
> And I shall conqueror be.

Chapter Eight

ACCEPTING GUIDANCE

THERE are few greater enemies of serenity than indecision. We all know the torment of soul which besets us when we have to make some choice which will have far-reaching effects for ourselves and those we love.

One day recently, while the American edition of this book was being prepared, I looked for a reference among my files. In doing so I came across a piece of paper I had forgotten. It was divided into four columns and in my own writing I had listed all the pros and cons of the options open to me in 1974. At that time I was minister of the Scots Church in Melbourne, the mother church of Presbyterianism in the state of Victoria. My wife and I had been there eight exciting years, but by 1974 the Scots Church people were divided over the proposed union among Congregationalists, Methodists and Presbyterians in Australia. (My wife and I believed in the union—now scheduled for consummation in June, 1977.) Knowing we were feeling unsettled, friends began opening doors for us elsewhere. We were pressed to go to another large church in the Melbourne area. Then came an invitation to consider a call to Western Australia. There was a third "sounding" to a church in Canada.

One day a letter came from Lowell Thomas, famous

81

author, explorer and newscaster asking us if we would consider moving to Quaker Hill, Pawling, New York. That seemed a long way away—10,000 miles—and would involve an enormous upheaval in our lives. From the family point of view we wanted to stay in Australia. On the other hand two daughters were living in North America with five of our grandchildren and that helped to balance things. Financially I would have been better off in one of the other positions, but in the ministry money is not the important factor.

Should we uproot everything and risk a "whole new ball game" at the other end of the world where our accent might not even be understood? As I had discovered in 1952 when we moved 600 miles from Melbourne to Sydney, our four children being then quite young, these decisions not only affect the lives of the two people most immediately involved, but they determine the whole future of others as well. We know all about the torment of indecision. But a line from the hymn, "Lead, kindly Light," kept running through my mind in 1974—

So long Thy power hath blest me, sure it still
Will lead me on.

We prayed about it until we were quite sure it was God's will for us to move to New York state. This conviction gave us the courage to make the plunge. We have always been happy in the ministry, but never more so than since we came to Pawling. Many exciting things have happened, and this book is one result!

In the catacombs, where the early Christians hid, the dolphin is represented among the symbols on the walls. Because dolphins frequently swim ahead of ships as though guiding them in the path they should take, they became the symbol of the friendly leader, and especially the symbol of Christ the guide. In ancient times the shepherd always walked ahead of his sheep leading them. So David sang, "The Lord is my shepherd . . . He leadeth me beside the still waters." Blessed are those who find the release from the torment of indecision and fear, by accepting the guidance of the Lord.

How does God lead us?—How do we know when the Lord is guiding us? May I give you a parable from Sydney Harbor? Our manse was near Rose Bay, the seaplane base. When a plane was due to arrive at night launches went out and laid down a string of floating lights in the direction of the wind. The lights also indicated a section of the harbor which was clear of yachts and other obstructions. As long as the pilot kept his eye on those lights, ignoring all other lights, and landed in line with them all was well. But if he said, "One light is good enough for me," and took his bearings from that he would have ended in disaster. God gives us common sense to guide us through life. Some people think that is enough, but it isn't. If we are wise we will seek the best possible advice. God often speaks to us through our friends, especially friends who have a concern for our highest possible welfare. But then two lights are not enough. I believe God often speaks to us in circumstances if we are alert to them. Then there are still more important lights. There is the Bible which is a lamp unto our feet and light unto our path. There is the centuries old experience and wisdom of the church. There is the wisdom of God mediated through the assembly of God's people met together in prayer. Above all there is the guidance of God's Holy Spirit given to those who humbly wait upon him in faith. As with Elijah it may not come to us in great things like the storm or the earthquake or the fire, but in the still small voice of conscience. If we are wise we will wait until all these lights point in the same direction and then we may know that whether or not it is what we want, it is the will of God for us and in the long run it will be much better for us and those whom we love.

It is natural to turn to God in the big decisions which overwhelm us and which make us realize our own lack of vision and weakness. Even Jesus knew the need to engage in lengthy prayer before the great decisions of his ministry, as when he chose his disciples and when he had to decide whether or not the time had come to give his life upon the cross. If he prayed before making his decisions, how much more should we pray? If we do, Jesus, who in his earthly life knew the torment of indecision, will lead us.

2

When does God lead us?—Just as the Good Shepherd leads his sheep in every movement that they make, so I believe it is right for us to seek guidance in trivial matters as well as important matters.

I had an aunt who lived beyond her ninetieth year. She was a most spiritual woman and she gathered round her a number of like-minded friends. One of these friends once left for a lengthy trip overseas. With everything to attend to in the rush and bustle of leaving, she was prevented from fulfilling one or two important duties. She was distressed about this and in due course she wrote a long letter to my aunt explaining what had happened. (I should explain that it was her custom to begin the day in prayer to God, seeking in that time of devotion to know what was God's will for her to do that day.) From her first port of call she wrote:—

"A bad trait in my character is indiscipline. So often I get qualms about things and people. 'Oh Goodness, I can't leave till this is done, or till I've seen so-and-so!' Then unexpectedly at the last moment things loom up and I try to fit this and that in, instead of sticking to the first things in the plan for the day. Will you please remember that failing in your prayers for me some time? It is a great drawback in my life and gives me unnecessary bustle which affects me physically. The days I adhere to the things in the day's plan, I find effortless, simple and have lots more time and leisure for the rest of the day."

To me it is a comforting and an inspiring thought that the Good Shepherd leads us in the trivial things as well as in the great things, and if we follow his leadership then he brings us out by the still waters, into the place of serenity. "Follow me," said Jesus. If we make him our pattern and accept the guidance of the Holy Spirit in all that we do then life takes on a new quality. Too many people make their decisions according to vague impulse or worse still according to prejudice rather than by principles. All the great people I know make their decision on facts and principles, being careful to leave out personalities and prejudices. The greatest make their decisions by seeking above all what is the will of God in their particular situation.

About 70 years ago in the little town of Pompton, some twenty miles west of New York City, a small boy set off early one morning in the week before Good Friday to go to church. It was a struggling little church, but a visiting preacher, remembered mainly for his red beard, had announced that he would conduct a service at 8 o'clock every morning of that Holy Week. The weather on this particular occasion was cold, wet and gloomy. When the boy arrived he found he was the only one present. He naturally concluded that the minister would not think of holding a service for one person and that a small boy. To his surprise the redbearded preacher went right ahead. In their service there was a place for responses by the congregation and the boy gave the responses. Not even the collection was omitted and after the boy had placed his dime in the plate the minister dedicated it. As he did so he placed his hand on the boy's head. After that he preached a sermon and then the service was over.

The boy grew up. Ever after he felt the touch of that hand on his head. He resolved to dedicate his talents to the service of God. He did not enter the ministry. He went to Hollywood and there he did something which made millions think more seriously about spiritual things. His name was Cecil B. de Mille. He had the courage to risk hundreds of thousands of dollars to put religion on the screen. He made "The Ten Commandments," "The King of Kings," "The Sign of the Cross" and "The Crusades." I can still remember the deep impression "The King of Kings" made upon me as a teenager. Nobody knows the name of that red-bearded preacher today, but many should be grateful to him that, when he had to make what might have appeared to be a trivial decision that cold morning (whether or not he should go on with the service when there was only a small boy present), that he made his decision in accord with the highest principles and the will of God.

Before we leave Cecil B. de Mille I feel I must record something else in his early life to show that the experience I have just described was not the only guiding light in his spiritual development. His father was a lay reader in the church and a writer of some ability. Each evening he used to gather the children round a big leather arm chair and read them stories from the Bible, one from the Old Testament and one from the New. He read them so well the children used to want more and more of them and, no doubt like most children, they were in no hurry to go to bed. They discovered that their father loved having his head rubbed and so Cecil was deputed to sit on the arm of the chair and gently stroke his father's head while the Bible stories went on. In this way they heard all the great biblical narratives, so that Cecil B. de Mille had a wonderful training in how to present the drama, the pathos, the humor and the glory of the Bible. The Bible is indeed a light unto our feet and a lamp unto our path. Blessed is every one who lights that lamp for a child. It is a guiding light that will never fail him to the end of his days.

3

Where does God lead us?—We have been emphasizing the need to make our decision in accord with the will of God. The way some people talk you get the impression that to say, "Thy will be done," is to invite something horrible to happen. Yet God's will is always for our highest and best welfare. In the long run he leads us into green pastures and beside still waters. For an outstanding example of that I can think of nothing better than Peter Marshall's romance.

Peter Marshall used to describe his conversion, which

took place in his early twenties, as the time when "the Chief touched me on the shoulder." Thereafter, with a quiet and simple faith he used to wait calmly for God to tell him what he was to do next. The film, "A Man Called Peter," powerfully portrayed this aspect of his nature, especially in the important matter of choosing a wife. The following account is taken from the film script by permission of Twentieth Century Fox and Mrs. Marshall.

At the age of 32 Peter Marshall was still a bachelor. Brought up near Glasgow he had migrated to America. After many difficulties during the depression he was enabled to work his way through a theological course and at the time of which I speak he was minister of the Westminster Presbyterian Church in Atlanta, Georgia. Catherine Wood was a twenty-year-old student in the Agnes Scott College. She was head over heels in love with Peter, but for two years he did not even know she existed. Then came the day when she was chosen to take part with two or three other students in a Temperance Rally led by Dr. Marshall. On the way home from the rally, Peter complimented Catherine on her part and so they fell into conversation. Anxious to find out whether Peter was heart-free or not, Catherine referred to rumors that he had a fiancée in Scotland. Other rumors said he had one in Atlanta. With some heat Peter replied, "I'll not get married until I'm good and ready. I'm good enough now, but I'm not ready," he added with a smile. Then growing serious he said, "If I can wait for the Lord to pick out my wife, why can't anyone else?" Catherine was shaken by that and said, "The Lord is going to do that?" "Why, certainly," said Peter with his rich Scottish accent. "And he'll pick you out for her?" queried Catherine. Peter replied, "Naturally. Don't you expect him to do as much for you? Maybe he has already? Well, if he hasn't, he will."

After a while Catherine reopened the subject saying, "Suppose you fell in love—without any encouragement from the Lord—and if you were head over heels and hopelessly in love?" Peter expressed his views in this way, "If it were really love it couldn't be hopeless. If it were the real

87

thing, a spiritual as well as a physical attraction, I'd know that sooner or later the Lord would take over. So I would just sit back and relax." Catherine thought that would be hard, but Peter concluded the subject by saying, "Miss Wood, Catherine, use that good head of yours. Who thought up love in the first place?"

By now they had reached the gate of the college and it was time to say goodnight. Solemnly shaking her by the hand Peter told Catherine he would call her up the next week and they would go to dinner and a movie. Apparently he was too busy to remember. It was the longest week Catherine ever spent. She resolved to go to another church, but sure enough the next Sunday she was back in her usual position. That day Peter Marshall preached on Marriage as "a oneness—divine and indivisible." After the service he took her for a drive. Saying goodnight to her that evening he told her he was off on a preaching and lecturing tour and would not see her for two weeks. Catherine's heart stopped. She had to tell him that this was really goodbye because she had almost completed her course and would be gone by the time he returned. Peter was startled, but merely took her hand again and wished her luck, saying he was sure she would be a very good teacher. This was too much for Catherine who turned and fled into the college.

Some little time later, when repeated buzzings on her bell had made no impression on the sobbing girl, the maid Emma managed to make her understand that Dr. Marshall had come back for her. As he took her in his arms he said,

"Oh, I am the stupid glaikit lump. I didn't realize what a shock this must be. God just spun me round like a top and said, 'Peter—you idiot—don't you see this is my grandest plan for you yet.'"

Sobbing now with joy Catherine clung to him and then drew away saying, "Peter, I'm frightened. Are you sure this is God's idea and not just Catherine Wood's. How could you know that for two solid years, from the first moment I saw you, I dreamed and schemed and plotted that somehow this would happen—that impossible as it seemed, you'd love me too."

"Catherine," said Peter, "this gets more and more wonderful."

"I don't know if it is," replied Catherine. "Maybe, you never had a chance! You hear about the power of thought, of willing things to happen."

We should all remember Peter's answer whenever we are tempted to think that to say "Thy will be done" is to invite something unpleasant. Peter said,

"Don't you know that God plants his own lovely dream in a human heart and when the dream in mature and the time for its fulfilment is ripe, to our astonishment and delight, we find that his will has become our will and our will his? Who but God could have worked out anything so perfect as this?"

So I believe God's purpose for each one of us is always something far better than we could plan for ourselves. Therefore if we make all our decisions according to the lights he has given us, if we seek his will and follow him, then each one of us will be able to say:

"He leadeth me beside the still waters . . . Surely goodness and mercy shall follow me all the days of my life: and I will dwell in the house of the Lord for ever."

Chapter Nine

ACCEPTING POWER OVER SIN

IN my mail one day I found an anonymous letter. It read as follows:

"I have been suffering a continual sin in my life for about two years. Although I am a Christian and have been praying about this I feel I have no power over it. Either I am not praying as I should, or I haven't enough faith that God will overcome it for me. Could you please make mention of it in your pulpit prayers as this is upsetting my whole life? I feel I am not worthy to ask God's forgiveness."

To this day I have no idea who the writer was, what was the nature of the sin, whether the writer was young or old, male or female. However, I did accede to the request and in spite of my inability to obtain the writer's permission to do so, I quoted the letter from the pulpit and then gave the following address on how to find power over sin. Two years later I received a New Year greeting card and on it an anonymous message. The writing was somewhat similar. I hope it was the same person because the message read, "Thanks for having helped me." Whether I am right in this guess or not, I certainly hope that what follows will now help many who are baffled with some sin which is exercising compulsive control over their lives. For many people some particular sin exercises a kind of fascination upon them. As soon as they begin thinking about it, the power of it spreads through their personalities and the more they try to screw up their will and fight it, the stronger this evil influence becomes. Like a bird hypnotized by a snake they flutter feebly, but soon give up the struggle. Putting it another way, repeated failures fill the sinner with the conviction that it is useless to struggle now. Since the moral struggle is torment, he yields to his sin to escape this torment, only to invite a worse torment in the long run. The Christian faith offers us an answer to this problem. Basically the answer consists in creating a situation in which the incidence of the moral battles is considerably reduced. When the battle cannot be avoided a power greater than our own power is available to those willing to fulfil the conditions and with faith to accept it. Consider some of these conditions.

1

A whole-hearted break with past evil.—Many of us want the power to win victory over sin, but we are not prepared to pay the price. The first part of the price is a whole-hearted repentance—a complete turning away from the past. It is not a bit of use hankering after the serene joys of the spiritual life and at the same time holding in our minds thoughts of the pleasures of sin. The sinful imagination will always beat us, the imagination being considerably stronger than the will. If we are whole-hearted in wanting God to remove from us our old evil nature, he can do it, but it requires first and foremost an act of will on our part.

The letter quoted above exemplifies another attitude that needs to be corrected. The writer was so weighed down by a sense of sin that he (or she) felt unworthy even to come to God in prayer for forgiveness. I have had others say to me in effect, "I'm not worthy to come to God. I'll have to wait until I get on top of this problem before I come." They don't seem to realize that if they could get on top of it themselves they would not need to come to God for moral power. The New Testament makes it abundantly plain that Christ does not expect us to come to him because we are worthy. Rather he calls us to come to him "just as we are," and he has promised, "Him that cometh to me I will in no wise cast out." Nevertheless Jesus does insist that we turn our backs on the evil past and follow him.

None of us can compromise with evil and get away with it. Look what happened to Samson who tried to do it. (This is one of the stories in the early part of the Bible which is half allegory and half history. These ancient people often wove allegorical stories around actual historical figures. They did so in quite good faith intending thereby to drive home religious and moral truths. The stories became so real to them that it is hard at this distance to decide where history ends and allegory begins. Nevertheless the eternal truths remain.) From his babyhood this phenomenally strong young man had been dedicated by his parents to a holy life. You would have thought that the least he could do would have been to have married a girl of his own religion, but instead he fell in love with a heathen Philistine woman. In spite of the heartbroken protests of his parents he persisted in his plans to marry her. At their wedding feast he put forth his famous riddle, "Out of the eater came forth meat, and out of the strong came forth sweetness." Unable to solve the riddle the Philistines prevailed on the bride to wheedle the secret from her husband. Physically strong as he was, Samson was but putty in the hands of a tearful woman. Having given away his secret he lost his temper and the final result was murder and a wrecked marriage.

Samson now had a double reason for keeping away from the Philistines. They were after his blood because he had killed so many of their people and their women had proved treacherous. But some strange fascination drew him back and, believe it or not, he allowed himself to fall in love with another Philistine girl, this time the notorious Delilah. Seeking to destroy him, but unable to do so because of his colossal strength, the Philistines prevailed on Delilah to extract the secret from him. Once more this strong man was like putty in the hands of a beautiful woman, and Samson fell again. He confided in her his conviction that his strength lay in his hair which had never been cut from the day of his birth. Then she caught him when he was asleep and with the help of a Philistine cut off his flowing locks. When he awoke he was as other men. The Philistines captured him and put out his eyes, making him a prisoner and a slave. It may be that the story can be explained psychologically, or more probably allegorically in the latter part. Be that as it may, let us lay to heart the great message it is meant to convey. No man can compromise with evil and get away with it. If we really want the victory, we must turn our backs completely on whatever may have caused our downfall in the past. It is highly dangerous to toy with evil.

2

A whole-hearted break with present evil.—Let us turn now to the second condition for victory over sin which is a whole-hearted break with evil round about us in the present. We live in a world which is full of evil influences and we cannot withdraw ourselves from the world. However, what is important is our habitual mental attitude and whether within ourselves we are really trying or only pretending. In the passage which attracted so much publicity during the campaign last year when quoted by President Carter, Jesus reminded men that the sin of murder began with the thought of hate, adultery with the thought of lust. That is where we have to fight our battle—in the mind. We must ruthlessly cut out of our lives everything that prompts wrong thinking. As the writer of a religious article in a newspaper once put it, "The answer to temptation is in prayer and flight." Perhaps that sounds cowardly, but it takes great strength of character to do it.

An excellent illustration of that truth is the story of Joseph and Potiphar's wife. This unscrupulous woman had fallen in love with the handsome and brilliant young Hebrew overseer of her husband's servants. She set out to seduce him and she made it all too easy for him to fall. It must have been a fearful temptation to a man in Joseph's position, but he was saved by two factors. On the one hand Joseph had trained himself to be constantly aware of the presence of God and of his own duty to God. When Potiphar's wife tempted him he replied, "How can I do this great wickedness and sin against God?" If we remember that all moral wrong is sin in God's sight, it changes our attitude to these things and gives us strength to fight evil. On the other hand Joseph got right out of the place of temptation. He fled from it. So let us avoid like the plague anything which would tend to put wrong thoughts into our mind and so start the chain reaction which ends in disaster. Let there be a whole-hearted break with present evil.

3

Whole-hearted acceptance of power over sin.—The third condition of victory is whole-hearted acceptance of power over sin. The writer of the letter at the beginning of this chapter no doubt believed in this power. As one claiming to be a Christian he had often prayed for it, but it is clear that he had not learned the art of calmly accepting it in faith. I don't say it is easy to learn that art. Some of Christendom's greatest saints were still learning at the end of their days. Nevertheless it is a reality as I learned from my association with various members of Alcoholics Anonymous. Repeatedly I came up against men and women who had made a complete wreck of their lives, and who, in spite of their earnest desire to break free, had gone on plunging from one awful defeat into another. No relief came until in simple faith they had learned the art of ceasing to rely on their own strength and accepting "the power greater than themselves." When they were prepared to admit they were beaten by the power of alcohol and, in humility, were willing to accept a power from outside themselves, then that power was given to them. I shall never forget one of the first members of Alcoholics Anonymous I came to know who sent an urgent message late one Sunday evening requesting me to visit him in his boarding house. When I arrived I found, to my great disappointment and distress, that he had "broken." For several months he had been "on the program" and, for the first time in fifteen years, had been enjoying the delights of sobriety. He had been one of our shining lights. Now he had slipped right back to the beginning. Perhaps, not quite right back, because although in one hand he held a bottle of gin, in the other he had a Bible. The Scriptures were open at the central portion of the book of Romans. He had been trying to read it for himself, but his eyes were now too bleary to make out the words, and he pleaded with me to read several chapters to him. As I did so I noticed a distinct change come over my alcoholic friend, particularly as I read the seventh and eighth chapters. By morning he was well on the road to recovery.

There isn't any question that there is power in the words of Holy Scripture. Jesus himself resorted to this power when he was battling with temptation in the wilderness following his baptism. The words of the book of Romans have often proved their power in lives of believers down the centuries. But it is a difficult book for moderns to understand. Let me try to express in present-day thought-forms what Paul is saying in the seventh and eighth chapters.

Paul tells us that he set off to be a good man. He had been brought up in a religious home and in the synagogue. He was taught the Scriptures, and he learned the Law of God. He believed that by keeping the Law man could be righteous in the sight of God and thereby know the blessedness of obedience to Him and the serenity of being right with God. Nobody kept the Law more faithfully than the naturally-religious Paul. He gave himself to it with enthusiasm, but instead of finding inner peace and moral victory, he found greater conflict and failure. In fact the Law made things worse. When it told him not to covet he began to covet though he had not thought of it before. The Law was actually putting thoughts of sin into his head. "Now, why should this be so?" Paul asked himself. "I don't want to sin, yet these wrong thoughts keep coming to me and the Law, which was meant for my protection, seems to be responsible. There must be an evil nature inside of me which makes me do the things I hate."

Paul attributed his evil nature to his inheritance from Adam. In more modern terms we might say that our human nature, which we inherit from our parents, grandparents and all who went before to the beginning of time, contains a large element of animal instinct. These instincts are often in conflict with one another and with our own nobler desires and impulses. Down the centuries the race has developed certain wrong attitudes and evil propensities. To some extent we have inherited these too. All this adds up to a force which inclines us towards evil in spite of our best intentions. "Who will deliver me from this power?" cries Paul. "Thank God, he will do it himself through Jesus Christ."

Against the evil propensity inherent in the race, God introduced an entirely new force for good with the appearance of Jesus Christ. He broke the fascination and the power of the old force for evil. More than that, believers may receive into their own spirits the spirit of the risen Christ. In a real sense Christ dwells in the believer and becomes a power within him. He cannot do that unless the believer is willing to "accept him." Thereby the Christian receives the moral power he needs. There can be no serenity for the soul constantly defeated by sin, but with him all things are possible.

One of the books which changed the history of Europe was Martin Luther's Commentary on "Romans," and especially his words on this theme. Like Paul, Luther had attempted to win righteousness and serenity by keeping all the laws of the church and, also like Paul, he had failed. However, while reading Paul's letter to the Romans, Luther discovered the answer. Luther comments, "Everyone discovers within himself aversion to what is good and a desire for what is evil . . . Scripture takes particular notice of the heart and of the root and main source of all sins, which is unbelief in the inmost heart . . . Faith is a divine work in us. Oh, it is a living, energetic, active, mighty thing this faith." So Luther goes on to show that faith leads to love and by love of God we delight to keep all his laws with our new, regenerated nature. Then we know the glorious liberty of the children of God, not because we are free of the Law, but because the Law of God now expresses how we want to act. We are at one with God and so at one with the laws of his universe when the spirit of Christ dwells in us.

4

Whole-hearted devotion in future. —One final condition must be stressed and that is whole-hearted devotion in the future. To hear some enthusiasts talk, all you have to do is to accept Christ and all your problems are solved for ever more. That is not true. It is a new battle every day. Jesus warned us we would need to take up our cross daily. To the end of life the struggle with temptation in one form or another goes on. We must plan our lives to make sure of victory in the future and begin with a regular intake of moral and spiritual power.

To that end it is essential that we keep with the right crowd. Just as a flight of birds moves as one because they are united at a deep instinctive level, so we are linked much more closely than we realize with the people round about us. George Williams in 1844 met a tremendous need when he resolved to form an association to take young men away from the degraded companions they were meeting night after night in the taverns of London and bring them into groups of Christian young men where the influences on their lives would protect them from temptation, rather than lead them into it. Today millions of men round the world give thanks to God for the protection of the Y.M.C.A. Not everyone is able to belong to the Y.M.C.A. today, but all of us can belong to the Christian church which, among many other blessings, provides a spiritual atmosphere which at once protects us from the sordid influence of the world and at the same time imparts greater moral strength to all who need it in the struggle against temptation. The church also helps us to discover the paradox that the more we share moral power the more we increase our own.

So let us, when the battle against temptation seems overwhelming and we are tempted to capitulate, remember there is One watching over us, One who loves us and who cares very much whether we win or lose. We are not alone in the fight. His Spirit can become our spirit. We are more than conquerors through him who loved us.

Chapter Ten

ACCEPTING GOD'S WORLD

DR. Leslie Weatherhead, during his visit to Australia in 1951, taught me a most valuable lesson. My wife and I had arranged to take him and his daughter Margaret for a picnic in the Dandenong Ranges about twenty-five miles out of Melbourne. We had chops grilled over an open fire and then drank "billy tea," tea brewed in a tin can. After that we went for a walk along bush tracks and country lanes. To me it was to be just another tramp in the hills, good exercise, fresh air and an occasional magnificent view, but how different it became with Leslie Weatherhead! He had trained himself to look for beauty in nature. He found beauty and he heard beauty in our Australian bush I had never even noticed before, let alone appreciated. I had heard magpies thousands of times, but now I heard their song through his ears and realized the glorious beauty of it. We are so used to gum-trees in Australia that we take them for granted. Leslie pointed out the glory of the sunlight glinting on the polished leaves of our despised Australian eucalyptus. Occasionally we would find a white gum or a towering mountain ash. As Leslie went into raptures about them, we could not help absorbing some of his enthusiasm. Then a flight of golden finches passed overhead wheeling this way and that in perfect precision. To others they were just birds, not worth a second glance. To Leslie it was sheer joy to watch them, controlled as they were by some "mass mind" if not "master mind," and again he drew our attention to the loveliness of the light glinting on their wings as they turned in the sun. That day Leslie Weatherhead explained to us that he had trained himself to look for beauty wherever he could find it. As he said, "You can draw strength from beauty."

Since that time I have proved it true in my own experience, but I have also found that we have to train ourselves before we reap any benefit. The mere existence of beauty round about us is not sufficient. Sydney Harbor is regarded as one of the most beautiful in the world. I can remember many times I looked out my window to see a glorious corner of it with the water reflecting the deep blue of a clear summer sky. Small steamers were always going by leaving white wakes behind while the further shore was green with gum-trees right down to the water's edge. Away from the harbor are many suburbs where there is no glimpse of the water, and little beauty at all. Yet in our church work we constantly found that the worst nerve cases and domestic tragedies are frequently found in the beautiful, wealthy suburbs with the harbor views. Possibly the beauty round about accentuates the tragedy when it comes. When people have not developed the right mental attitude natural beauty does not prevent nervous collapse or domestic tension. It is a solemn thought that the people who travel out to the Gap (the high cliff near the South Head of the harbor) to commit suicide, travel what is probably the most beautiful route in Australia. When the mind is darkened by mental and spiritual trouble, physical beauty is little help.

When that has been said, I am convinced that the cultivation of the right mental and spiritual attitude toward beauty can do much to build up strength of spirit. It is no accident that so much of God's world is sheer beauty. I am sure he intended us to cultivate a mental attitude towards it which is based primarily on our faith in him and in his goodness. If we

learn to accept God's gifts and God's world in the right spirit
and thereby cultivate a habit of joy in them and gratitude for
them, we build up a healthy and positive attitude of mind
which works for harmony and serenity within and consequently releases vital forces in the personality. As Paul said
to Timothy (1 Tim. 6:17) trust not "in uncertain riches, but
in the living God, who giveth us richly all things to enjoy."

1

Uncertain riches.—Some years ago a man said to be the
richest in the world lay dying—in misery. His name was
Gulbenkian, his age was given as 86 and his fortune was
estimated at $1,400,000,000. He possessed an art collection
worth $60,000,000, and he owned a ton and a half of pure
gold. Yet for years he had lived in deep depression of spirit.
An Armenian by birth he had, no doubt, suffered considerably from poverty in his youth. In any case he became
obsessed with the desire to make more and more money.
Eventually he secured an interest in a substantial proportion
of Middle East oil wells. He knew the British wanted to gain
control of the Iraq oil-fields, and he helped them do it—for a
consideration. All he asked was 5% of the profits. It sounded
reasonable enough, but it added up each year to an enormous
amount. So Gulbenkian made a fortune, and he used it to
make still more fortunes. If money could buy happiness and
serenity, Gulbenkian should have been the happiest and
most serene man in the world. Was he? For the last fourteen
years of his life he lived in a three-roomed suite in a hotel in
Portugal. He rarely went out for fear of meeting people
wanting a loan. He could not bear the sight of beggars. He
was convinced somebody was going to shoot him or poison
him. All his food had to be tested before he would eat it.
Whenever he did go out there was always a guard watching
over him. For all his wealth he lived in constant terror of his
life. He had long since forgotten what serenity or happiness

were like. Yet the humblest child of God who has learned to love and appreciate the beauty of God's universe is richer than Gulbenkian ever was without any danger of his mind being darkened by fears.

Serenity can't be bought with money, but it can certainly be destroyed by a wrong attitude to wealth and God's gifts generally. No one denies that a certain amount of money, under modern conditions, is desirable for serenity. We need it for the normal necessities of life, and without those necessities life can be dreadful. But to assume that because some money buys some serenity a lot of money will buy a lot of serenity is to make a tragic mistake. It is then that we become obsessed with something which only enslaves us. One of the best things about church stewardship campaigns is that they set people free from that slavery. As Paul puts it, if we have the simple necessities of life like food and clothing, let us be thankful and trust God for the future. Then we can concentrate on living a Christlike life, pursuing not sordid gain, but the good of others and the kingdom of God. When that happens the personality is set free from restrictive influences and begins to grow. A great sense of freedom and a deep satisfaction follow.

Many rich men are turned in on themselves. Being rich they are tempted to think they are free from normal moral standards. They imagine their wealth will always give them power over others. So they become more and more tense, disillusioned and depressed. Christianity takes the strain out of life by saving us from this false goal and by giving us a new ideal which meets the highest needs of the personality. The kind of people we are and the happiness we find depend to a great extent on that in which we put our trust. So I turn to the second point Paul makes.

2

Trust in the living God.—When I went to Britain to do a post-graduate course, I decided to see the country by pedaling a bicycle from London to Glasgow. The first day out I resolved to call on an old lady in whom my family had been interested for many years. In trying to find the hamlet in which she lived I found myself cycling down the lanes of Essex, lanes so narrow that when a farmer's cart came toward me I had to press myself into the hedge at the side to allow it to pass. Dog-roses growing in profusion through the hedges and the glory of the English trees were a constant joy. Eventually I found the cottage. A tiny but perfect garden surrounded it. Inside the beams of the ancient ceiling were so low I felt I had to bow my head to walk across the room. As I greeted the old lady I thought she looked a picture of dignity and serenity. At the same time she was a bright and happy soul. A black kettle was simmering on the hearth. Beside the big open fireplace was an ancient tapestry and on the mantelpiece were photographs of several generations of her family. She herself had never married and had lived alone in this cottage for many years. But she was not alone. On a little table beside her arm chair was a well-worn Bible. She lived on a meager pension, but she was rich in a way Gulbenkian had never dreamed of being rich, because she trusted in the living God. To her he was not a God who existed in somebody's imagination centuries ago, but a living God, alive and powerful and real today. So many people believe in God with their minds, but they live out their lives as though there were no God. Not so with Aunt Emily. To her God was intensely real, and she trusted him with a calm and serene faith to look after her day by day and on into the future. When the war came and enemy bombers roared overhead on their way to London night after night, her faith held firm. She was an inspiration and a strength to her neighbors. She was a serene old lady, and her secret was a practical trust in the living God. Thousands trust in God when things are going well, but their faith evaporates when things don't go as they think they should. The real test of trust in God is when we can still hold on however black the horizon and still believe that through it all he is working out some loving purpose which we don't understand now, but which we will understand one day. The true serenity comes to those who firmly believe that all things do work together for good to them that love God, and live their lives by that faith.

3

God, who giveth us richly all things.—God in his infinite wisdom has not only provided for us the simple necessities of life, but he has made them very good so that we may enjoy even the most elementary of them.

Take air, for example. We all need air and can't survive without it, but how often do we realize what a grand thing it is? Richard Aldrich in the biography of his wife, Gertrude Lawrence the actress, describes how they first met. He, as a theatrical producer, called for her at a country station and then drove her through the night to the place where she was to spend a short vacation. On their way through the country she asked him would he mind if she were to open the window of the car. Holding her face to the opening she said, "How divine it feels! So cool and clean and good. Do you know what I would like to do? Get out and walk in it for miles and miles." Fresh air is good, isn't it? And Gertrude Lawrence was right. It is "divine"—a gift of God.

Or take fresh water. In the jungle in New Guinea during World War II, I swore that if ever I could get back to a place where I could go and drink a cup of cold water whenever I wanted it, or bathe in a proper bath, or eat fresh meat, or walk on a carpet I would never complain about anything else.

When Admiral Richard E. Byrd lived alone through an Antarctic night within 10 degrees of the South Pole he discovered the truth of our Lord's saying, "A man's life consisteth not in the abundance of the things which he posseseth." Actually we can get along with very little. Byrd came to see that success in life consists in being content with a few material things and then seeking harmony in ourselves and in our family circles. Having attained serenity in himself Admiral Byrd tells us that he felt more alive than ever before. He wrote, "A man's moments of serenity are few, but a few will sustain him a lifetime."

When the Rev. Murdo Ewen MacDonald of St. George's West Church in Edinburgh preached in Australia, he described conditions in a prisoner of war camp where he had been held. A piece of bread became so vital that cultured officers would fling self-respect to the winds and fight for it. Today while millions of the human race still hunger for bread, we have all we need. How often do we thank God for such a simple thing as bread? If we remember to be thankful for simple things we won't be nearly so worried about luxuries that don't really matter.

St. Francis discovered that secret. The son of a wealthy cloth merchant, Francis squandered his father's wealth with dissolute companions. Strangely enough his father did not object since the others were sons of aristocratic families and he thought his son was making valuable contacts. Then Francis had a change of heart and began to spend his money on the needy. The father was incensed and haled the young man before their bishop for discipline. Francis asked to be excused for a few minutes from the interview. He returned wearing a plain robe. He handed back his rich apparel, his money and jewelry to his father declaring that from that moment he was married to poverty. No doubt Francis was exceptional, but for the rest of his life, though he lived in a penniless state, he was one of the happiest men the world has known revelling in the glories of nature, in the birds, the flowers and all the good gifts of God.

There is one other good gift of God which too often we take for granted—the gift of human love. When we have it we treat it as though it is something we possess by right, or something which in some way we have deserved. But what a wonderful gift it is! A man once wrote to me describing a critical illness which had overtaken his wife. Her life was hanging by a thread and then pneumonia set in. It seemed that nothing could save her. Naturally he prayed and as he prayed he did some stock-taking. He thought with shame of the habit he had fallen into of finding fault with many of her ways, losing sight of the good she had done. He realized that this fault-finding had not only caused her considerable hurt, but it did himself great harm. He resolved that if his wife were spared to him, he would thereafter treasure her as a great gift from God. I am glad to be able to say that she did survive the crisis, and I'm quite sure theirs is a much happier home today.

4

All things to enjoy.—There is a final thought in regard to this matter which I must stress. As Paul emphasizes, God has given us all things not merely to keep us alive, or to use for some other purpose, but to enjoy. God means us to find joy in living, and the more we find, the more strength comes to us and the longer we live. The human machine is working efficiently at all three levels, spiritual, mental and physical when there is joy and joy helps it to work more efficiently.

One day I called on an elderly member of my church. I found him reading Einstein's *Theory of Relativity.* For years he had been manager of a large wholesale pharmaceutical firm, but his spare time was spent in scientific studies. He took me into a large room filled with charts, coils, valves and gadgets of all kinds. One wall seemed to me to be nothing but an immense black space. Going behind a piano, Mr. Hector pulled a switch and then began to play. As he pressed a key there suddenly appeared in what I had taken to be empty black space, a beautiful forest scene. As a scientist he had linked together that particular note and the color red. He pressed a different note and I heard a new sound while the color blue flooded the scene I was watching. A third note changed the light to gold and so on. When chords were struck some wonderful lighting effects were produced. I found myself being deeply moved by this extraordinary combination of light and sound, and I was not surprised to be told that when a group of spastic children had spent an afternoon watching and listening a definite healing influence had been detected in them.

Mr. Hector, whose work with color-sound is referred to in the *Encyclopedia Britannica*, tells me that the inspiration came to him when he was worshiping one day in our church. As he listened to the organ he was gazing up at the colors in a stained glass window, and the thought came to him that it would be a wonderful thing if the colors could change with the sound. So he evolved his amazing aparatus. Perhaps it helped to keep him young. It has certainly kept him interested in life, and, in spite of several bereavements and much frustration, enjoying life. He lived to be over 90 years of age. One of his favorite hymns was "For the beauty of the earth" by F. S. Pierpoint and particularly the verse—

> *For the joy of ear and eye,*
> *For the heart and mind's delight,*
> *For the mystic harmony*
> *Linking sense to sound and sight,*
> *Christ, our God, to Thee we raise*
> *This our sacrifice of praise.*

We all need to learn to appreciate the beauty of God's world and to enjoy it. When we do, strength, spiritual, mental and physical, is released in us.

Chapter Eleven

ACCEPTING CHRIST

THROUGHOUT this book our theme has been that serenity depends on a certain mental attitude—an attitude which accepts and gives rise to spiritual power. We have to train ourselves to appreciate the good gifts of God, material, mental and spiritual. Among all God's gifts there is none greater than Christ himself and in this chapter I want to discuss what is really meant by the expression "accepting Christ." Those who properly understand this experience and enter into it are the ones who know what the deepest serenity is, but how many do understand and enter in?

When I was in my late teens I had a friend who was concerned about my soul. At the time I had announced my intention of entering the ministry and was studying toward that end. My friend thought I was spending far too much time in the various school activities, out on the oval and down at the river. I allowed myself to be persuaded to attend the meetings of a fiery evangelist in a nearby church. At the conclusion of an impassioned address the evangelist challenged all those prepared to "accept Christ" to stand up. I knew my friend beside me was praying hard that I would stand and I certainly felt an inner urge to do so, but I couldn't do it. I don't think it was lack of courage. Some years later I did stand before a congregation and make confession of my faith. It was not a very terrifying experience.

Thinking it over afterwards I came to the conclusion that the main thing holding me back that night was the conviction that if I did stand up it would not be honest. It wasn't want of loyalty or faith, but it was an unhappy feeling that I did not understand what was meant by the expression, "accept Christ." Did they mean, "Accept him with the mind, believing that he was the Son of God who was crucified on Calvary and who rose again from the dead?" I believed that, but obviously more was needed. Did they mean then, "Accept a new way of life following his example and based on faith in him?" It had long seemed obvious to me that religion was little use unless it made some difference to the way you lived. I was quite prepared to consider a new kind of daily conduct. There was ample room for improvement. At the same time I felt the standards set by this particular evangelist were so absurdly narrow and restrictive that they could only produce warped personalities with little resemblance to the divine personality of Jesus. Deep down in my soul I knew that more than this was involved in the experience of "accepting Christ," more even than accepting him with the affections and loving him. Boy-like I found it difficult to love someone I had never seen, though I was still prepared to try. It was not till many years later after a lengthy study of the New Testament that I discovered what it really means to accept Christ.

The key to the whole mystery is in the word "spirit." As we saw in an earlier chapter, he is spirit and we are spirit. If we are willing to receive his spirit into our spirits, to be identified with him, then life can begin again and we are, as it were, "reborn." He is the spirit of life. New life and strength, love and glory come to us when we "accept him." This is essential New Testament doctrine. Paul wrote to his friends at Ephesus saying (3:17) "I pray that Christ may dwell in your hearts by faith." To these ancient people the heart was the center of the thinking, the will, the personality. When the spirit of Christ is in control there, then there are certain important results. Among many others there are three named here by St. Paul, strength, love and glory.

Strength.—The Christians at Ephesus were like a good many people today. Their faith held strong until they met adversity. Then, in the hour they needed it most their faith crumbled. Why? Because their faith was built on the false and selfish attitude that if you serve God, he will protect you from harm and bring you blessings. The believers at Ephesus were in real difficulty because they knew Paul was in prison because of his faith. He was suffering on their behalf and this seemed to them altogether wrong. Why did God reward him like this? Paul knew the situation was bothering them, as it had bothered him in the past, but he had found the answer and he now tried to convey it to them. Amid worldly affliction it is possible to find a spiritual calm and strength which is far more important than any transitory material or physical prosperity or adversity. Paul wrote to them saying he hoped they would discover this truth and telling them that he was praying for them that they might be "strengthened with might by his Spirit in the inner man." He goes on, "that Christ may dwell in your hearts by faith." Later in the same third chapter he refers to "the power that worketh in us."

That power is still a great reality in the lives of all true believers. Several years ago a girl I know became engaged to a young man whom she had known for several years. A few days after their engagement was announced the young man was taken to the hospital where it was found he was suffering from leukemia. For thirteen weeks he lived on blood transfusions. Then he was allowed to go home, but a few days later he had to return to the hospital in a worse condition than ever. Indeed, the doctors feared that he would not live through the night. His fiancée was a religious girl, and she prayed for a miracle. Next day she felt sure the miracle had happened. A noted philanthropist, Sir Edward Hallstrom, had given $10,000 for experiments with the wonder drug A.C.T.H. Used on the young man the drug had a dramatic effect and he lived for another fifteen months. Then he began to sink again and in spite of everything that could be done he passed peacefully away. Several years later his fiancée wrote me a letter telling the story and she used these words, "I went to the hospital every night, and I know it was only through God that I had the strength to carry the burden. The day he died I felt God had placed a cloak over my shoulders for protection. I have never experienced anything like it in all my life." That spiritual experience gave her strength to face her sorrow and through it to gain a purer and more reliable faith. Some time later she met another very fine young man, and I had the pleasure of performing their marriage service. They worshiped regularly with us from that day on. The strength she found was an inward, spiritual strength. She knew it was not her own strength. It had come to her from "outside." It is the kind of strength given to those who accept Christ in the heart.

In chapter nine we dealt at length with this strength as applied to the problem of temptation. It is not necessary to go into detail again on this point, but it might be interesting to quote in the present context what Paul wrote in the 10th verse of the 8th chapter of Romans, "If Christ is in you, although your bodies are dead because of sin, your spirits are alive. . . ." J. B. Phillips paraphrases this section as follows, "You cannot be a Christian unless you have something of his Spirit in you. Now if Christ does live within you his presence means that your sinful nature is dead, but your spirit becomes alive." There is undoubtedly a "power that worketh in us" available to all who sincerely wish to conquer temptation and who are willing to "accept Christ" by faith.

2

Love.—Returning to the third chapter of Ephesians we note that Paul says, "that Christ may dwell in your hearts by faith; that ye being rooted and grounded in love may be able to comprehend with all the saints . . . the love of Christ." Because his spirit is the spirit of love we can tell when people have it. They are more loving.

Down the centuries this effect of the spirit of Christ on ordinary men and women has produced some of the shining chapters in the history of the church. Because of it the unfortunate and the wretched, those who are despised and rejected by the rest of the world, have found help and, what is more important, love. One thinks of the lepers helped by Damien, the poor assisted by Francis, the orphans befriended by Barnardo, the prisoners loved by Elizabeth Fry and John Howard, exploited children helped by Shaftesbury and the unevangelized cared for by such men as David Livingstone and Albert Schweitzer. In line with this great tradition is a story which only came to my notice recently.

Some sixty years ago in the city of Sydney there was a Jewish gentleman who had been converted to Christianity. His name was George Lewis and in his spare time he gave himself to lay preaching and mission work in the Liverpool Street area. He obtained his normal livelihood from government service and in due time became the first Commonwealth Electoral Officer. However, his main interest was in bringing the Christian gospel to the afflicted and the needy. His mission work in those days was under the auspices of the Pitt Street Congregational Church. In the course of his work in caring for the poor he came across two girls who both had the same sordid story to tell. They were "in trouble" and did not know which way to turn. George Lewis talked the matter over with some of his helpers and finally decided to take over, apparently out of his own resources, a cottage in the suburb of Annandale. There he installed a fine young Christian lady by name Henrietta Attenborough who undertook to care for the two girls. The immediate crisis had been met, but it was not long before other girls were hearing of what had been done and were turning to them. As has happened so often in the past, that which began as a temporary measure became a permanent institution. Miss Attenborough stayed on to care for hundreds of these unfortunate girls. It was said of the Queen Victoria Home, as it was called in those days, that there was often great financial need but always "a wealth of love." From my own impressions of some of the girls who have had to go there in recent years, I would say that there was nothing they needed more. They had been driven into a wayward life by a lack of love at home. In their hunger for it they had turned in the wrong directions. I know how they have been helped to find the right path again by the atmosphere they have found at the "Queen Vic." George Lewis bequeathed the property to the Presbyterian Church. When he died, the home was in a bad state of repair and the church faced many problems in the years that lay ahead. However the main difficulties were overcome. It has become a general maternity hospital with an excellent name. At the same time the George Lewis block continues to cater for the work so dear to his heart. In our highly organized churches of today it is difficult to preserve the direct personal contact, but at least the sinews of war can be provided by those congregations moved by the spirit of Christ. There is still room for personal service. The love which such people bring to their service is something they have found by "accepting Christ." It is that love which performs miracles in the lives of those who are too often treated as outcasts by the rest of the world.

3

Glory.—There is another significant word which Paul uses when discussing this subject of accepting Christ and that is the word "glory." He uses it in his epistle to the Colossians, "Christ in you, the hope of glory." In this passage Paul refers to the "mystery which hath been hid from ages and from generations" which is now revealed as the loving purpose of God to lead mankind into a new and glorious existence when they find they can receive the spirit of Christ himself into their own personalities. As the Apostle John put it, "in him was life." In the eighth chapter of Romans Paul wrote, "If the Spirit of him who raised Jesus from the dead dwells in you, He who raised Christ Jesus from the dead will give life to your mortal bodies also through his Spirit which dwells in you." At the worldly level we share in the mortality of all physical things. "Change and decay in all around I see," said Henry Francis Lyte when he knew his own life was drawing rapidly to a close. But Christ is eternal. If we accept him and receive his spirit into our spirits, then we share with him the wonder of eternal life. Not only do we receive a new vitality in this life, but in the world to come life everlasting.

Has it ever occurred to you to ask why the communion service, which is such a baffling mystery to the uninitiated, has retained its central place in the worship of the church for nineteen centuries? To some casual observers it appears such a simple thing as to be devoid of any real significance or power. Yet it has been spiritual meat and drink to millions because it expresses in an outward and visible form the spiritual reality of "accepting Christ." Bread is regarded as the "staff of life." Christ becomes our spiritual life when we accept him. The prayer "that Christ may dwell in your hearts by faith" is answered every time we come to communion "in spirit and in truth."

Whether we do it at a communion service or in a simple act of humble faith and worship let us accept Christ afresh, receive his spirit into our spirits. Plainly His spirit being a pure and holy spirit cannot live with that which is impure and unholy. We must be clean. We must repent and turn from our selfish and evil ways. Nor can he come in if pride keeps him out. Naturally we want to run our lives. We don't want anybody else taking control. But are we so good at running our own lives? Why should we be afraid of letting him take control? He is the king of love and far wiser than we are. All who accept Christ prove that he is their inward strength. He is the spirit of love and he is, in us, the hope of glory.

Chapter Twelve

THE SECRET WITHIN THE SECRET

THE parable of the two seas is now well-known, but its message is so important that I want to repeat it here by recalling my own impressions of the Dead Sea and the Sea of Galilee. I travelled to Jerusalem by train and arrived in the late afternoon. Finding the Church of Scotland Hospice near the station, I deposited my bags and made my way at once to the flat roof to drink in my first impression of the holy city. It was a thrilling sight with the Mount of Olives towering behind. Away to the right was a yawning valley, too deep for me to see the floor of it. Beyond was a range of hills, purple in the gathering twilight, the mountains of Moab.

A few days later I took a bus down into this valley. It was exciting to see the Inn of the Good Samaritan. Later I had a queer feeling as we passed a notice saying SEA LEVEL, when it was obvious that we had many hundreds of feet to descend yet and still no sign of water. As we reached the floor of the valley and turned the shoulder of the hill towards the Dead Sea I thought I had never seen anything so arid in my life. (Some miles to the right were the caves in which the Dead Sea Scrolls were later discovered. This was the rocky plain where in 1969 Bishop Pike perished of thirst.) The water was shimmering white in the intense heat and round the shores were acres of white salt. Beyond the salt no vegetation marked the brown earth or the cracked walls of the surrounding valley. I went for a swim and, as expected, I found it difficult to sink. The water is so full of salt you feel your head and shoulders are standing out of it all the time. Unfortunately I had dived in and the salt made my eyes sting so much I was glad to come out. I was not surprised that fish soon perish in water of the Dead Sea or that birds give it a wide berth.

A week later I journeyed some eighty miles to the north and when I first caught sight of the Sea of Galilee the beauty of it took my breath away. Here and there trees came down to the water's edge. The city of Tiberias and a number of villages clustered round the water. Fishing boats were out among the fish, still plentiful after centuries of exploitation. The song of the birds above the fresh blue waters was a joy to hear. This was a sea of life. The other was a sea of death. What makes the difference? The same Jordan water flows into each. The difference is that the Sea of Galilee receives to give again, the Dead Sea keeps everything and gives nothing. So it is with human lives.

A member of my church said to me one day, "Nothing we have is ours to keep. It is only lent to us for a time to use for others." The beauty and serenity of her life made me realize that she had discovered a wonderful secret of living.

The same truth was brought home to me during a preaching and lecturing tour of New Zealand. At the suggestion of the organizers I spoke in Auckland and Wellington, Christchurch and Dunedin on several subjects including spiritual healing. In each case I told the story of the healing which had come to me when I was threatened with a major operation in regard to a spinal condition. (The full story is told in the final chapter of my book *The Blessing of Belief.*) I was embarrassed as I spoke in public of something which was very personal, but I felt it my duty to give thanks to God for his healing and at the same time I was anxious that others might be helped to a true understanding of the spiritual forces available to the sick. Frankly, I expected to have trouble on that trip. As anybody who has had severe back trouble knows, over-tiredness is a sure way to bring back the pain. Furthermore I was involved in a trip of over 4,000 miles in 11 days, I had to sleep in a number of strange beds and at the same time to fulfill a great many public and private engagements. If my back had collapsed altogether it would hardly have been surprising. Instead of that it seemed to gain strength. As I flew back to Australia, I asked myself why this should be so. Then I remembered that Jesus made it perfectly plain that spiritual blessings are not given for our own selfish use or enjoyment of them. They are to be shared with others and the more we share them the more they are increased to us. "Give and it shall be given unto you." On the other hand hoard to yourself the good gifts of God and they go bad.

The Apostle Paul discovered this power, this secret within the secret of how inner peace and serenity of soul might be found. In the first chapter of his letter to the Christians in Rome he wrote (verses 11, 12): "For I long to see you; I want to bring you some spiritual gift to make you strong; or rather I want to be among you to receive encouragement myself through the influence of your faith on me as of mine on you," (New English Bible).

The great thing about our Christian faith is that it lifts us out of ourselves and widens our horizons. There is no quick-er way to destroy serenity than to become obsessed with self. The word "idiot" comes from the Greek word for "own" or "private." The more we become wrapped up in our own affairs the more likely we are to lose our balance, our seren-ity, our sanity. The more we can lose ourselves in the love and service of others the stronger and more serene we be-come. The great thing that Christ does is to save us from ourselves.

Forgetfulness of self takes much of the tension out of life. The best way to forget self is to be really interested in others.

If we have found serenity then our Christian duty and high privilege is to share it with those who are still seeking for it. In doing so we bring blessing to them and at the same time confirm this great spiritual blessing to ourselves. Let us accept this principle and live by it.

From beginning to end of our search for spiritual peace and power one word has kept recurring again and again— "accept." I have tried to show that the important thing is to develop a new mental attitude—an attitude which accepts things we cannot change in the past, present and future, an attitude which accepts people we cannot change—above all an attitude which accepts the good gifts of God. What an astonishing, constantly available power this is, the power that comes to us through spiritual acceptance.

1. Do your best to eliminate from your life everything which disturbs your peace.
2. Ask God to give you serenity.
3. Believe that he has done so.
4. Affirm that you now do have "the peace of God which passeth all understanding" in your soul.
5. Make a deliberate attempt to help somebody else find peace.

The Serenity Prayer makes clear the dynamic power of Christian *action* and Christian *acceptance*:

The Serenity Prayer:

> God grant me serenity to accept the things I cannot change, courage to change things I can and wisdom to know the difference.   Amen.

EPILOGUE—EXAMPLES OF
POWER THROUGH ACCEPTANCE

1.

Donald was an artist. In his early twenties, doors were opening for him to develop his considerable talent. Then came the war, and he went off in the army, leaving behind a newly-married wife. Donald, the artist, hated life in the army. For him the war was dreary, uncomfortable, sometimes dangerous, and interminable. Then came word that his wife had gone off with somebody else.

That was when Donald developed his drinking problem. By the time he returned home, his cultured parents scarcely recognized him. He was rough, tough and aggressive. Because his drinking was now out of control, he was unable to hold any position for very long. His long-suffering family stood by him, but increasingly he found it difficult to cope with life. He still had his artistic talent, but his ability to produce pictures of real quality had disappeared. Donald became more and more depressed.

Then Donald fell in love again. Cecille was a fellow artist, and she believed in him. But when Donald proposed marriage she declined. She admitted she loved him, but she was afraid of him when he was drunk. She saw no future for either of them unless he could control his drinking. Such was Donald's regard for her, he made a really heroic effort and for

119

months lived an exemplary life. But then he broke and things were worse than ever. Cecille had repeatedly urged him to join Alcoholics Anonymous, but each time he refused saying he had all the will-power he needed to run his own life. Now he was desperate enough to try A.A.

At his first meeting Donald was very ill-at-ease. He found it hard to suppress his contempt for some "no-hopers" as he called them, men and women who had recently joined and who were still showing the effects of years of problem drinking. Then he realized he was just as much a "no-hoper" as they were. Before the end of the evening he was admitting that though they looked sick, they were not without promise. In fact that was the only thing some of them had. Donald felt a new challenge, new hope.

How did it come to him? For one thing there was the group therapy. He was mixing with people who could say, "I know how you feel. I've been through all that." Then, too, he sensed, as A.A. phrases it, the "Power Greater than Yourself." He had to admit that relying on his own will-power he had failed again and again, as others had. But now this strange "Power" had enabled them all to do what they had not been able to do on their own. Where did they get it? Many of them seemed to put great emphasis on the words of the "Serenity Prayer" (here, and above in Chapter Five, is my paraphrase of the lines by Reinhold Niebuhr).

God grant me serenity to accept the things I cannot change, courage to change things I can and wisdom to know the difference.

Serenity to accept! That is the key to freedom from tension, to peace of mind and the release of power.

For years Donald had been saying to himself and others, "But for the war I could have been the greatest artist in the country. But for the war my marriage would not have ended in disaster." He had built up an enormous amount of resentment against people who had rejected him when he was under the influence, against employers who had dismissed him because his work was not up to standard, against the wife who had deserted him. Now he realized that all these unhappy things were in the past and not all the bitter feelings in the world could alter them. He was only hurting himself.

When he sincerely asked God to give him the serenity to accept these things, to his surprise and relief he found this blessing was granted. A weight seemed to roll off his shoulders. He began to feel free again. He sensed a new power to cope with life. Once more he became creative.

In due time I had the joy of performing the marriage between Donald and Cecille. Since then Donald has become an outstanding artist, and he is keeping sober.

2.

Dr. W. L. Northridge, the British psychologist, once described a young woman acutely conscious of the fact she was not beautiful. She was sensible enough to try all the regular beauty aids and these helped, but it was obvious she would never qualify for a Miss Universe competition. Standing before her mirror one day she said to herself, "If I can't be beautiful, I'll be kind." She accepted the fact she was not destined for a life of glamor. At that point she, too, experienced a feeling of relief. She was released from fears and resentments which had held her back. As she put into practice her new resolution, power began to flow into her and through her to others. It was power by acceptance. Understandably she became a much-loved person.

3.

Some years ago I travelled on the same ship with a writer whose works were being read by thousands of people round the world. We were traveling through the tropics and most passengers were content to laze away the time in deck chairs. You could usually see Hector in such a chair either reading a book, or more often asleep with the book resting across his face. But one day when we were all looking forward to putting into one of our ports of call on the morrow, Hector was missing. At lunch he told us he had spent the morning writing an article which he would airmail to America when we pulled in next day. It took my breath away when he casually mentioned that he expected a fee of $1000 for that one article which would be syndicated through a number of newspapers. In those days where I came from, a fee of $20 was considered big time.

But what surprised me even more was to meet another passenger on that same ship, a lady, who had known Hector in school. He was the despair of all his teachers. He had no capacity for fitting in with the normal school system. With unfailing regularity he gravitated to the bottom of class after class. Finally they put him in a special class reserved for "problem children." There were 46 in that class and Hector worked his way down to 37th position. The despair of his teachers, he was also the despair of his parents who were convinced he would never do anything worthwhile with his life.

But Hector had one talent, writing, and he was determined to use it. He was wise enough to accept the fact he would never shine at mathematics, physics or indeed any subject which involved an examination. He knew his limitations and accepted them. He refused to worry about them. He got on with what he could do. As he did so, more and more power came to him to be creative in the field he had chosen.

Donald was eking out a miserable existence, a problem to himself and those who loved him, till he came to the point where he found serenity to accept his past. At that point he ceased to use up his mental and emotional resources fighting against it. The forces of his personality were now focused on an attainable goal and he had a new sense of power flowing through him. He became creative again.

The young woman described by Dr. Northridge found power to enjoy life and help others enjoy it when she stopped rebelling against her homely looks.

Hector's life could well have been blighted by his consistent record of failure in school. But finding his true metier he accepted all those failures mentally and emotionally and enjoyed himself immensely doing the one thing for which he had a flair.

4.

As I type these words in 1976, the movie, "The Hiding Place," is being screened all over America. It depicts the true story of Corrie and Betsie ten Boom who were sent to a Nazi concentration camp for harboring Jews in Holland. In response to inhuman conditions others sank to the level of animals, but Corrie and Betsie, with firm faith in God, came to accept even the fleas which protected them against sadistic guards. So they were given power to witness and bring comfort to their fellow sufferers.

5.

A friend of mine, at the age of 57, lost his job when his firm's business was affected by the prevailing economic recession. At his age he was afraid he would never find another position. In a half-hearted manner he applied for three different positions and each time was rejected. For weeks his spirit was broken. His wife worried because he was so depressed and seemed to be losing the incentive to make any further attempts. He spent much of his time sitting round the house and complaining of the state of the world. Not only the economy, but the whole country was going to the dogs in his view.

One day, knowing I was making a broadcast, he turned on the radio. In a brief devotional message I said (not realizing he was listening), "God never shuts one door without opening another." He got up immediately, amazed his wife by telling her he was going out to get a new job, and cheerfully kissed her goodbye.

At lunchtime the telephone rang in their home. When the

wife answered it, her husband told her he would not be back until evening. He had already started work in a very congenial position, a position which proved better than the one he had occupied for so many years previously. No doubt his faith and cheerful attitude made a difference in the crucial interview that day.

His success was made possible by his willingness to accept the past and not be bitter about it. At the same time the radio message reminded him that God still cared. He could hand over his emotional burden to God as he worried about the future. In that moment he accepted the "peace of God which passeth all understanding." As serenity returned to him, power was released in him.

6.

It is possible to think of many examples from American history. Abraham Lincoln could have spent his days rebelling against life because of the loss of his mother in early childhood, poverty and the lack of education, the treachery of a business partner who bankrupted him and left him to pay off their creditors, the betrayal by certain political supporters and so much else. But Lincoln was big-hearted and big-minded. In 1862 he appointed one of his greatest enemies, Edwin M. Stanton, to the position of Secretary of War because, he said, he was the man best fitted for the job.

Lincoln did not complain because life had given him a raw deal. He accepted it. But some things he refused to accept because they blighted the lives of others. He refused to accept slavery. And he was strong enough to win the victory against slavery because he had won the victory against negative emotions in his own soul.

7.

Franklin Delano Roosevelt's policies cause debate in some circles to this day, but surely no one can fail to admire his victory over paralysis. To the end of his days he had to accept it, to live with it. But he did accept it. He did not allow it to defeat his spirit.

8.

The famous evangelist, Wilbur Chapman, was once so weary and so disheartened in his work at a big church in Philadelphia that he wrote out his resignation, intending to return to secular employment. He did that early on a Monday morning and then went to eat his breakfast. In doing so he picked up the *New York Tribune* which contained reports of sermons preached the previous day. That day there was a summary of the sermon preached by Dr. F. B. Meyer and in it was a sentence which seemed to hit Wilbur Chapman right between the eyes:

"It does not so much matter what we do for God; but it matters a great deal what God does through us."

Chapman threw down the paper and said, "I see it. I have been trying to work for God, but now I am going to let God have a chance." Then right there at the breakfast table he prayed saying, "O God, here is my life, work through it as Thou wilt."

It was the turning point in a wonderful life. If ever power entered a man's personality, it did that day. In the years that followed as Chapman teamed up with Alexander, thousands of people were won to the Kingdom of God, including some of my own relatives in far off Australia.

It takes faith to accept power from God. He has made it clear that the power does not flow if we harbor in our hearts resentment, hatred, bitterness, fear or anxiety. If we are prepared to hand these things over to God, praying for serenity to accept the things we cannot change, the power begins to flow.